QUALITY IMPROVEMENT
IN CONTINUING HIGHER EDUCATION
AND SERVICE ORGANIZATIONS

QUALITY IMPROVEMENT IN CONTINUING HIGHER EDUCATION AND SERVICE ORGANIZATIONS

Edited by
Paul F. Fendt
and
G. Michael Vavrek

The Edwin Mellen Press
Lewiston/Queenston/Lampeter

Library of Congress Cataloging-in-Publication Data

Quality improvement in continuing higher education and service
 organizations / edited by Paul F. Fendt and G. Michael Vavrek.
     p.   cm.
  Includes bibliographical references.
  ISBN 0-7734-9220-8
  1. Total quality management. 2. Universities and colleges-
-Administration. I. Fendt, Paul F. II. Vavrek, G. Michael.
HD62.15.Q356 1993
658.5'62--dc20   92-40882
                                                                       CIP

A CIP catalog record for this book
is available from the British Library.

The Edwin Mellen Press   The Edwin Mellen Press
       Box 450   Box 67
  Lewiston, New York   Queenston, Ontario
     USA 14092   CANADA L0S 1L0

                    Edwin Mellen Press, Ltd.
                    Lampeter, Dyfed, Wales
                  UNITED KINGDOM SA48 7DY

            Printed in the United States of America

TABLE OF CONTENTS

G. Michael Vavrek
Deming's philosophy and 14-point methodology, a basis for Japan's post-WWII
economic turnaround and now accepted widely by American business and industry,
are applicable to the service sector.

Paul F. Fendt
When comparing two "fathers of significant movements," one from business and
industry, the other from adult education, striking commonalities are found.
Although their work was conceived apart and for different audiences, both Deming
and Knowles sound the same notes with mature learners.

Lorraine A. Cavalier
Deming provides processes for land-grant universities to adopt a new quality philosophy to deliver improved products and services to the many diverse constituents
of the complex organization.

Jerome F.E. Halverson
Private continuing higher education seems to be more naturally compatible with
Deming's principles but all systems resist change.

Rick P. Williamson
The economic development roles of community colleges and businesses are entwined by the need for ever-improving quality.

Walter A. Cameron
The organization's journey to service quality is rewarding for customers and employees. This chapter presents examples of how service companies are improving
quality and suggests a model for ensuring continuous improvement.

J. Michael Lewis
Service and administrative organizations require the same key element for successful implementation of quality management -- strong leadership.

Public school systems must deal proactively with the expanding perception that quality management can improve even public education.

A critique of Deming shows how his means of delivery inhibit reception and illustrates the incompleteness of the message because it does not consider culture.

Quality improvement programs are successful because they have a system and implement it rigorously. Leadership is the key to being passionately systematic. A leadership model and Deming's points are integrated.

FORWARD

"Higher education could learn from industry . . . management, planning, evaluation, and accountability." These words, from UC-San Diego's Mary Walshok at the National University Continuing Education's forum on corporate/campus collaboration, speak to what non-industrial organizations might glean from W. Edwards Deming. He, an American, is credited with engineering Japan's post-WWII economic turnaround. This source book examines the applicability of the Deming way to improve quality in continuing higher education and other service organizations. While Deming is accepted widely by American industry, his ideas are just beginning to impact the service sector. Therefore, readers will be better able to envision the application of his assertions to their settings by thinking of educators as service providers and students as customers.

Chapter One is the foundation for a detailed examination of the fitness of the Deming way . The emergence of Deming, the meanings of quality, and Deming's fourteen obligations of management are discussed. Deming's points are referenced to Scherkenbach because he explains Deming very clearly.

The striking commonalities that connect Deming and Malcolm Knowles are identified in Chapter Two. By describing the parallels of behavioral and psychological intent of both leaders, we start to see the utility of Deming to adult education theory and practice.

In Chapter Three Lorraine Cavaliere discusses the first of three post-secondary institutional types that could consider applying the Deming way. The bureaucratic complexities of massive land-grant universities are analyzed.

The private university is the next context for testing the usefulness of Deming. In Chapter Four Jerry Halverson focuses on only a few obligations but he aims them very specifically at classroom issues.

Rick Williamson, in Chapter Five, compares the community college to American business from the viewpoint of economic development. He draws some of Deming's points into common themes that link community colleges and businesses around the quality improvement purpose.

Walter Cameron, in Chapter Six, describes five examples of service organizations that are using quality improvement programs; this is a rare collection vi

because the service sector is only beginning to explore the philosophy and methodology.

How to improve the American public schools? By telling the story of the Kingsport, Tennessee school system, Charles Tollett shows, in Chapter Eight, that the quality-oriented methods of business work.

John Dew, in Chapter Nine, critiques Deming by showing how his means of delivering inhibits receptivity to the message and illustrates the incompleteness of the message because it does not consider culture.

Chapter Ten is an integration of a leadership model and Deming's points.

This source book grew from an NUCEA/Continuing Higher Education Leadership, Kellogg-funded professional development project: "The Blue Ridge Continuing Higher Education Exchange Network." It introduced eleven continuing education leaders from Northeast Tennessee, Southwest Virginia, and Northwest North Carolina to the Deming way. The editors directed that project. A special thank you goes to Michael Lewis, Coordinator - Quality Management, Holston Defense Corporation, Kingsport, Tennessee. His expertise in the Deming way provided the knowledge and skills for the successful completion of the training project.

ACKNOWLEDGEMENTS

The editors wish to acknowledge the devotion of the chapter authors: Walter A. Cameron, Professor, Department of Technological and Adult Education and Director, Office of Human Resources, University of Tennessee-Knoxville; Lorraine Cavaliere, Director, Continuing Education, Pennsylvania State University - Great Valley Campus; John R. Dew, Training Manager, Martin Marietta, Paducah, KY; Jerome F.E. Halverson, Dean, New College, University of St. Thomas, St. Paul, MN; J. Michael Lewis, Coordinator, Quality Management, Holston Defense Corporation, Kingsport, TN; Charles Tollett, Senior Program Associate, Center for Creative Leadership, Greensboro, NC; and Rick P. Williamson, Associate Professor and Director, Continuing Education, Wytheville Community College, VA.

The editors also appreciate the outstanding manuscript preparation assistance of Karen Bowes, Berwick, Pennsylvania.

Finally, the editors recognize the support of their home institutions. Paul F. Fendt is Director, Mon Valley Tri-State Leadership Academy, West Virginia University. G. Michael Vavrek is Dean, School of Extended Programs, Bloomsburg University, Pennsylvania.

CHAPTER ONE

AN AMERICAN LEADS THE JAPANESE
AND THE U.S.A. FOLLOWS
G. Michael Vavrek

Deming's philosophy and fourteen-point methodology, a basis for Japan's post-WWII economic turnaround and now accepted widely by American business and industry, are applicable to the service sector.

The pervasive concern related to improving quality is fulfilling management's responsibility to exercise leadership for the comprehensive and constant improvement of the system plus the on-going development of people as individuals and teammates; this is the essence of W. Edwards Deming's philosophy and methodology. This chapter provides the foundation for a detailed examination of how the Deming way can apply to quality improvement in a sample of continuing education and service organizations. In setting the stage for learning lessons about the Deming way, this chapter answers these questions: Who is Deming? What does quality mean? What are the key concepts of his philosophy? What happened in Japan? What is happening in America? What are Deming's fourteen obligations of management?

W. EDWARDS DEMING

Deming's work as a statistician for the government's Census Bureau in the 1940s led to his first trip to Japan in 1948. The Japanese took a deep interest in his statistical methods which eliminated inspection and made quality everybody's job. Meanwhile, the United States ignored acute focus on quality because the post-

WWII national and international demand for "made in America" goods mandated emphasis on quantity.

To understand the Deming way, one must know something about the person. Born in 1901, he received his doctorate in mathematical physics from Yale University in 1928. A world-wide consultant for over forty years, he has been a professor of statistics at the Graduate School of Business Administration of New York University since 1946 and distinguished lecturer in management at Columbia University since 1985. Clients of his consultancy range from railways to research universities, from manufacturing companies to hospitals.

Some of his awards are: 1956 Shewhart Medal from the American Society for Quality Control, 1983 the Taylor Key Award from the American Management Association, 1986 election into the National Academy of Engineering and the Science and Technology Hall of Fame, and 1987 the National Medal of Technology.

Deming's breadth of interests include having written two masses and several canticles and anthems.

MEANING OF QUALITY

Few people will argue against the importance of quality, but what does it mean? As preface to considering the key specific concepts of Deming's quality philosophy, let us mull over different meanings of quality.

Garvin's (1984) examination of the translations of product quality identifies five approaches. One, the philosophers' transcendent path concludes that quality is synonymous with innate excellence, unanalyzable properties that are recognized only after many experiences. Two, economists say quality is a precise and measurable variable of the attributes possessed by a product. Three, the user-based approach of economics, marketing, and operations management views quality as the extent to which a product or service satisfies the expectations of a consumer. Four, the manufacturing-based definition means the degree to which a product or service conforms to a design or specification. Five, the value-added road leads to quality being the amount of excellence at an acceptable price and the control of variability at a fitting cost.

In light of these definitions, Garvin names eight dimensions of quality: performance, features, reliability, conformance, durability, serviceability, aesthetics, and perceived quality, along with four correlates of price: advertising, market share, costs, and profitability. Given these definitions and correlates, Garvin concludes that an organization that chooses to compete on the basis of quality can do so in several ways by selecting one or more of the elements as the aim of its niche.

DEMING'S QUALITY PHILOSOPHY

Contrary to the impression given by Deming's statistical background, his is not just an application of numbers to the work setting. He has developed a new concept of how to manage systems, a whole new philosophy of management. The basic idea is that if management is to be responsible for improving something as complicated as an organization, managers must have a way of learning what parts of the problems are due to the workers and what parts are due to the system.

Deming believes that two circumstances must be fulfilled if managers are to learn. First, workers and managers must speak the same language--statistics. Although we use numbers (a.k.a. statistics) every day in a multitude of ways, Deming recognizes that even among educated people there is a tendency to shun statistics (a.k.a. numbers) that can tell us how much variation is unusual. If variation is to be controlled and higher quality achieved, Deming believes managers and workers must communicate accurately using the language of statistics. Second, management must use workers as essential "instruments" in under-standing what happens at the work site. In contrast to the prevailing American way of taking the system as a given and working harder to get the most out of it, the Deming way advocates people working smarter. Management's job is to provide leadership in working smarter to improve the system by enabling workers to provide insights into how to improve output and efficiency. A changed managerial self-image is imperative.

JAPAN LISTENED AND ACTED

After WWII the Japanese listened to Deming, but Americans did not. Japan was conquered and its economy in ruins. Smaller than California but with a population half the size of the U.S.A., Japan faced a monumental challenge with very few natural resources. Japanese industrialists had the limited objective of wanting to bring their country back to its pre-WWII level.

In 1946 commander of U.S. Occupation Forces in Japan General Douglas MacArthur also wanted rapid improvement, but his subordinates disagreed on how. His Economics and Social Section objected to a training system that had proven successful with the Japanese, saying that it might be too successful. The Civil Communications Section (CCS), which had conducted the training, believed that it would be more practical to teach the defeated and starving nation to be self-sufficient. MacArthur agreed with CCS.

Thinking that quality meant making half of your products okay and throwing out the other half, the Japanese seemed to know little of modern management or production techniques. Homer Sarasohn and Charles Protzman, of the CCS, taught a course for top Japanese managers that emphasized "the social mission of the enterprise as the objective of the enterprise" along with these key points: first, need for each company to have "a concise, complete statement of the purpose of (its) existence, one that provides a well-defined target for the idealistic efforts of the employees"; second, the company must put quality "ahead of profit, pursuing it rigorously with techniques such as statistical quality control"; and third, all employees deserve "the same kind of respect fellow managers receive, and good management is democratic management" (Wood, 1989, p.71). Aided by the MacArthur government, the Japanese Union of Science and Engineering invited Deming to tell them about quality control. After studying the Japanese work force and its habits Deming was convinced his methods could be applied. Meeting at his invitation, Deming told Japan's top 45 industrialists that if they applied his methods, within five years Japan would be an important factor in international trade. Despite their more limited objective of wanting to return to pre-WWII levels and their disbelief of Deming, the industrialists did not want to lose face. So they tried his ideas. Within six weeks there were reported productivity gains of up to 30 percent without new equipment. Japanese industrialists realized Deming's way worked and began devoting their time and energies to it.

The reverence with which Deming is held in Japan is indicated by their awarding the annual Deming Prize, the most coveted industrial honor in the country. Winning it is a national event, reported on national television.

Today Japanese management has further developed by adding exclusively Japanese elements, for example, the work of Masaaki Imai, author of Kaizen, The Key to Japan's Competitive Success (1982). "Kai" means change, "zen" means good (for the better). Put together, Kaizen translated to gradual, continual improvement: doing little things better; setting and achieving ever higher standards.

AMERICA IS LISTENING AND ACTING

The evolution of managing for quality in the U.S.A., especially during the 20th century, is worth a synopsis. The tradition of independent master craftsmen changed with the Industrial Revolution, although quality was still managed through the skills of craftsmen retitled inspectors. The Taylor System of Scientific Management that separated planning from execution, while increasing productivity, crippled the concept of craftsmanship by relying on inspectors to prevent defective products from being sent to customers thus hampered efforts to eliminate the causes of poor quality.

The massive cutback of civilian wares during WWII resulted in huge shortages amid a giant buildup of purchasing power after the war. Production quantity far overshadowed attention to quality as upper management became detached from the process of managing for quality.

While the U.S.A. was focusing on quantity, Japan embarked on a course of reaching national goals by trade, not by military means. Since shoddy goods were their trademark, they adopted a variety of strategies for creating a revolution in quality that emphasized the personal involvement of upper managers, training at all levels for all functions, and improvement at a continuing, revolutionary pace as the basis for competing on quality, not on price. During the 1960s and 1970s American/Japanese competition changed from price to quality as Japanese manufacturers dramatically increased their U.S.A. market share. In the early 1980s many American upper managers noticed the trend and responded by implementing strategies such as quality circles, statistical process control, computation of cost of quality, and incentives for quality.

America is learning that quality competitiveness in the 21st century is far more likely with a new basic approach designed to call for organization-wide quality management which focuses on enlarging the strategic plan to include quality goals and the personal involvement of upper managers. Training for all must be emphasized in order to accelerate the current, unacceptably slow pace of quality improvement. Planning must emphasize participation of internal customers and the use of a systematic approach. Quality control must emphasize conditions for worker self-control, define responsibility for critical decisions and actions, and coordinate multifunctional processes.

America is acting. In 1988 Motorola earned the first annual Malcolm Baldridge National Quality Award, named for the former Commerce Secretary. Motorola told its suppliers to apply for the Baldridge Award or lose Motorola as a customer.

In 1989, both Xerox and textile manufacturer Milliken & Co. earned the Baldridge Award, presented by President Bush, who declared high quality a top national priority. Xerox earned it again in 1990.

Excellence is a matter of corporate survival as indicated by the fact that "more than 80 percent of the consumers surveyed (in 1988) said that quality was more important than price. In 1978 only 30 percent said so. An estimated 87 percent of the largest U.S. industrial corporations have expanded their quality-enhancement programs during the past two years . . . Another measure of corporate interest in quality: 40 colleges and universities now offer degrees in quality technology, up from nine in 1986" (Castro, 1989, p.79). The change in corporate philosophy and operations is being recognized as increasingly vital as competitive challenges from abroad grow. Joining with Japan are Germany, much of Asia, the European community, Mexico, and Brazil.

The quality concern is expanding beyond manufacturing. The fall 1987 edition of The Quality Review, published by the American Society for Quality Control and the nation's leading publication on quality management, features Kingsport, Tennessee and Madison, Wisconsin as premier examples of applying quality management to the public sector. Kingsport's Quality First training program, which employs the philosophy and methods of Deming, helped a variety of local government, business, and civic organizations save $3.2 million during the first nine months of implementation.

Education is also the focus of quality management efforts. A 1984 National Institute of Education report, "Involvement in Learning: Realizing the Potential of American Higher Education," was among the first to charge that "quality and focus are slipping" in U.S. higher education (Time, 1984, p.78). Among the indictments were: lack of adequate ways to assess student learning, mass lectures for freshmen, faculty teaching less than full-time, poor academic advising, and excessively vocational curricula.

The 1989 comprehensive appraisal of management education done by the American Assembly of Collegiate Schools of Business cited such "dangers (as) letting programs proliferate without adequate attention to quality control." There also was found among corporate America a lack of "the critical intensity that such as Peter Drucker, W. Edwards Deming, or Tom Peters have expressed about fundamental failings in managers' . . . concern for quality and workmanship" (Dill, 1989, p.56).

DEMING'S FOURTEEN OBLIGATIONS OF TOP MANAGEMENT

The pervasive concern related to improving quality is fulfilling management's responsibility to exercise leadership for the comprehensive and constant improvement of the system plus the on-going development of people as individuals and teammates. This distillation of the Deming way says that it means not just an application of statistics to the workplace but rather a new concept of how to manage.

1. **Create Constancy of Purpose Toward Improvement**

"Create constancy of purpose toward improvement of product and service, with the aim to become competitive, stay in business, and provide jobs" (Scherkenbach, 1988, p.9; he is an outstanding interpreter of Deming).

To initiate change, an organization needs a long-range plan based firmly on a fundamental view of its basic character or mission. Although based on assumptions about societal trends, the process of conducting business must start with the customer. The essential steps for any business have traditionally been design it, make it, and sell it, but Deming adds the fourth step--test it--, the provider and the user and potential user must communicate. Operationally defining customers' needs throughout the organization forms the basis for constancy of purpose that Deming urges; only top management can get at it by making policy, establishing a set of core values, and determining the long-term course. The latter factor points to Deming's emphasis on the long-term results, not short-term as has dominated America. We are in a new economic age where many competitors "are not compromising the future to the extent that we have been . . . Constancy of purpose affects the opportunities of tomorrow. But the course needs to be set today" (Scherkenbach, 1988, p.12 & 13). Doing our best is not good enough.

Knowing what to do is establishing the constancy of purpose; doing our best means maintaining consistency of purpose.

2.   Adopt the New Philosophy

"Adopt the new philosophy. We are in a new economic age, created by Japan. Western management must awaken to the challenge, must learn their responsibilities, and take on leadership for change" (Scherkenbach, 1988, p.15).

A philosophy is basically a set of assumptions about the nature of reality. Former thinking related to quality improvement was that higher quality costs more. A good manager set up a system, directed the work through subordinates, made unambiguous assignments, developed work performance standards, and evaluated employees accordingly. However, this assumption does not work in the new economic age characterized by the philosophy that higher quality costs less.

After the war Japan was receptive to Deming's new philosophy, their only resources, people and willing management. Japan has created a new economic age; America is losing an economic war. However, signs now indicate that America is receptive to the new philosophy that higher quality costs less because it requires less reworking.

3.   Cease Dependence on Mass Inspection

"Cease dependence on inspection to achieve quality. Eliminate the need for inspection on a mass basis by building quality into the product in the first place" (Scherkenbach, 1988, p.25).

The Deming philosophy is that higher quality costs less because less reworking is required. Putting the new philosophy into operation mandates that the processes or systems used to achieve the output be managed so that quality development occurs continuously. At the same time we must accept that variability is inevitable especially in people-dominated processes. Although many people probably agree, they expect near perfection in their daily affairs because that is quality. The Deming way challenges us to be open minded to the possibility that our management methods might not get the desired results.

Detecting defects is not a viable strategy; the waste of overcontrol occurs because management does not understand that the world is variable. Continuous improvement is the Deming way.

4. Improve the System Constantly and Forever

"Improve constantly and forever the system of production and service, to improve quality and productivity, and thus constantly decrease costs" (Scherkenbach, 1988, p.35).

The Deming cycle for continuous improvement consists of four steps with the customer always the target: plan, do, check, and act. First, recognize the opportunity by operationally defining it and operationally defining a theory that forms the basis for a rational prediction. Second, test the theory in a laboratory or real setting, on a small scale, with actual customers. The theory could start with a hunch or a law of nature or physics, but Deming points out the important element to remember is "the only purpose of collecting data or conducting an experiment or test is to form the basis of a rational prediction" (Scherkenbach, 1988, p.38). Third, observe the results, using any quantitative or qualitative method that could affect the ability to predict results. Fourth, act on the opportunity pointed out by the test results; this returns the process of continuous improvement to step one, of recognizing the opportunity.

Each step in the Deming cycle is critical because the four are inter-dependent. Traditional learning teaches us that some level of performance is good enough, but Deming says continual reduction of variability is possible. However, a "truly competitive improvement can be made only if management has the flexibility to increase costs in some area. History is replete with examples of society accepting the accumulation of small losses and rallying to avoid one large loss which, in reality, might be smaller than the total of the smaller losses" (Scherkenbach, 1988, p.42 & 43).

5. Remove Barriers

"Remove barriers that rob the hourly worker of his right to pride of workmanship. The responsibility of supervisors must be changed from stressing sheer numbers to quality. Remove barriers that rob people in management and engineering of their right to pride of workmanship. This means the abolishment of the annual merit rating and of management by objective" (Scherkenbach, 1988, p.47).

Deming has always said that "it is management's sacred responsibility to counsel and develop its people . . . (to maintain) deep regard for people and recognize that employees are the organization's most important resource . . . principal purposes of an appraisal and development system should be to nurture and sustain individual employees' contributions to the continuous improvement of the organization as a team and to provide an assessment of performance for the employee and management" (Scherkenbach, 1988, p.57). But Deming sees common performance appraisal systems as the biggest inhibitor to pride and consequently to continuing improvement: they destroy teamwork, foster mediocrity, increase variability, confound people and other inputs, and focus on the short-term.

Teamwork. Since most organizations are functionally oriented, sub-unit objectives relate to the different jobs; this system usually leads to mutually exclusive goals with the boss being the employee's most important customer. Other customers and teamwork are short-changed in the win-lose environment. Higher education is no exception: "in most universities (evaluation procedures) stifle teamwork since the procedures make it difficult for people to work together for the good of the university" (Cornesky, 1989, p.130).

In contrast, Deming emphasizes a three-part process for developing group objectives: outcomes, process, and inputs. Outcomes are the group objectives that bind employees to meeting customers' needs. Group focuses on others outside one's own organizational sub-unit; objectives must emphasize meeting customers' needs, not an intermediate result defined by a self-limiting number. Synergy is vital. The process for developing group objectives flows from identifying customers' needs, to determining possible sources of improvement, to recognizing who can help accomplish improvement, to developing mutual objectives. Concern for inputs requires an understanding of the sources of variability: people, equipment, materials, methods, and environment.

Mediocrity. Functionally-oriented organizations use attribute-type appraisal: the objective is either achieved or not. When fear of failure permeates the organization, it reduces initiative and risk-taking because mediocre objectives result from the negotiation process. In contrast, Deming promotes focusing on continual improvement.

Variability. Prevalent appraisal systems cannot define operationally the difference between adjacent categories, e.g. outstanding high and outstanding; this ineffectiveness is compounded by the finding that "a major failure of performance reviews is an inability of managers to communicate with subordinates about their strengths and weaknesses" (Scherkenbach, 1988, p.52). "Management by exception" also contributes to variability because it brings special cases to the manager. In contrast, the Deming Way says that managers should work on helping corrective actions continue. Managers must understand that variability is natural and then use all means to continually work on reducing significant variation.

6.   Drive Out Fear

"Drive out fear, so that everyone may work effectively for the company" (Scherkenbach, 1988, p.75).

Scherkenbach asserts: "I personally don't think that fear will ever be driven from the workplace. It is everywhere and . . . in many forms (of which some) can be helpful . . . especially in the beginning stages of transition to continuing improvement . . . Fear is the antithesis of Dr. Deming's philosophies, but apathy and short-term myopia were an even bigger roadblock" (1988, p.75). Managers asking the right questions about continuing improvement can cause subordinates to seek answers. The key is management's willingness to learn. However, Deming observes that fear of knowledge pervades many levels of management; in turn, it reduces competitiveness because of sluggish response to change. The Deming way means continual improvement through continual learning.

Trust based on communication aids learning and improvement; this may be acutely applicable in higher education as focused on by Cornesky's (1989) application of Deming to higher education. Among his observances are these: "an academic unit without trust cannot thrive . . . . trust provides the foundation (for) integrity, leaders should trust themselves without letting their ego or image get in the way (p.86), administrators must realize that communication creates meaning for people, and that through it, people can become aligned behind the goals of the university" (p.103).

7.   Break Down Barriers Between Departments

"Break down barriers between departments. People in research, design, sales, and production must work as a team to foresee problems of production and use that may be encountered with the product or service" (Scherkenbach, 1988, p.79).

The Deming way requires operationally defining the customers' critical characteristics throughout the organization as the basis for removing barriers to continual improvement. As with driving out fear, trust is critical to ousting barriers.

We must face reality when considering the Deming way's applying to education and perhaps some service organizations: "The differences between administrators and faculty members in role expectations, goals, and even personality characteristics often contribute to interpersonal conflict" (Cornesky, 1989, p.91). However, Deming's challenge is still valid: get everyone involved, recognizing that they each have something to contribute and they can do so in an atmosphere of mutual respect.

8. Eliminate Numerical Goals

"Eliminate slogans, exhortations, and targets for the work force that ask for zero defects and new levels of productivity" (Scherkenbach, 1988, p.83).

Deming asserts that managers seem to operate on the premise that individual employees are solely responsible for outcomes; many times other resources dominate the employee's influence on the outcome. While slogans and so forth may increase awareness and generate motivation, nothing substitutes for training, knowledge of the process, and tools and methods to manage the process. In education, "Management's supposition that faculty can improve their course grading without meaningful training, better prepared students, or up-to-date equipment and facilities indicates that management lacks leadership" (Cornesky, 1989, p.117).

9. Eliminate Work Standards

"Eliminate work standards (quotas) on the factory floor. Substitute leadership. Eliminate management by objective. Eliminate management by numbers, numerical goals. Substitute leadership" (Scherkenbach, 1988, p.85).

Deming believes that these impede quality more than any other single working condition because "work standards tend to cap the amount of improvement that can be achieved" (Scherkenbach, 1988, p.86). The figures used for planning should not be scientifically fixed and/or politically negotiated but should emerge from listening to the result of the current process. Work standards also confuse people's understanding of exactly what their job is. Is it to accomplish so many "whatevers" per time period (process) or to meet customers' needs? The challenge is to hear both in the feedback loop. By hearing only the process feedback, management may lose the customer. But by concentrating only on the customer, management may lose production because of increased costs. Leaders that listen and act to continually improve the system are essential.

10.   Institute Modern Methods of Supervision

"Institute leadership. The aim of leadership should be to help people, machines and gadgets do a better job. Supervision of management is in need of overhaul, as well as supervision of production workers" (Scherkenbach, 1988, p.89).

The new economic age requires managers to be coaches and teachers. Their prime job is to develop people so that they can always be improving. Managers must be enabled to manage people first, things second. This does not require just getting back to basics because a "rogue element" (Scherkenbach, 1988, p.90) is involved: new choices, possibilities previously nonexistent. Applied in the education context this, in part, means: "It is not the intelligence, education, life styles, or backgrounds of either administrators or faculty that constitute truly successful institutions; it is the ability of the administrators and faculty to effectively deal with each other" (Cornesky, 1989, p.76).

11.   Institute Modern Methods of Training

"Institute training on the job" (Scherkenbach, 1988, p.91).

Let us consider training from the perspective of what inhibits it and what statistical tools are needed to achieve continual improvement.

An interesting contrast to the American situation is the Japanese management's view that the training budget is the last cost-cutting area "because training and education are the cornerstones of greater consistency" (Scherkenbach, 1988, p.91). However, American companies generally are increasing their training expenditures; if so, why has training not been more effective? Management has not changed systems to use the training because of these inhibitors.

Inhibitors

Statistical training is for my people, not me. The Deming way clearly requires that management, as well as technicians, understand statistical thinking because most of the improvement is in their hands.

It is for manufacturing, not me. Training in statistical thinking is just beginning to develop nonmanufacturing examples of application; this is vital because if it is to be successful, a broad range of applications must be demonstrated, especially in the service sector.

Our problems are different. Deming's approach is based on the view that all processes are generically the same.

We rely on experience. Deming says, "If experience taught us something, why are we in such a mess?"

Hope for instant pudding. Currently managers are short-term oriented. For example, Deming often gets calls asking him to go to a company for a day and do what he did for Japan. No shortcuts or simple "fixes" can solve complex problems. Quality improvement is the synergistic effect of an integrated system.

Statistical Tools

A broad understanding of statistical thinking and tools undergrids the Deming environment for continuing improvement. All employees must have it.

Before going further let us recognize that this section only briefly introduces the statistical tools of the Deming way. These books should be consulted for greater detail: Deming (1951 and 1982), Ishikawa (1983), Western Electric (1954), and QIP Inc. (1984).

As a final foundation for considering the tools, we must clarify the terms enumerative and analytic situations. *Enumerative* study evaluates numerical characteristics of a situation. The aim of an *analytic* study is to discover causes and how to modify the process. Substantive knowledge (engineering, psychology, medicine, agriculture, consumer research) bridges the gap when enumeration and analysis differ. "In making any decision you must balance your knowledge of the subject matter with your knowledge from statistics. It is rarely either/or" (Scherkenbach, 1988, p.98).

Control charts enable many other statistical tools to be used in this world, not only the theoretical world, because they prove the lack of applicability of some theoretical assumptions such as randomness, equal variance, and independence of outcomes. Special and common causes of variation are examined. The former, not common to all operations, is the responsibility of someone directly connected with the process; the latter, the opposite, is management's job.

Flow diagrams enable a depiction of a process in as much detail as wanted.

Cause and effect diagrams force people to think explicitly about the specifics of processes. This effort also encourages teamwork, builds a list of improvement opportunities, and focuses on reasons for variability.

Histograms are effective only for data that comes from a process in statistical control because they display distribution of individual outcomes.

Pareto diagrams are used to focus on the most important opportunities for improvement which are commonly 20 percent of the possibilities. The "80/20 rule" means that 80 percent of the improvement comes from 20 percent of the possibilities. The question to remember is not to rank first and last among the possibilities, but who or what is inside or outside the system.

Scatter diagrams are used to examine possible relationships among data which are unrelated to cause and effect.

Graphs enable management to quickly see trends without pouring through reams of precise numbers.

Design of experiments is a vital Deming way tool once a process is in control. Real improvement can start because experiments enable management to plan and analyze more than one variable at a time, a process necessitated by today's problems with their complex interactions between factors.

12.   Institute a Program of Education and Retraining

"Institute a vigorous program of education and self-improvement" (Scherkenbach, 1988, p.125).

As the Deming way takes hold in an organization, fewer incoming resources are used because waste decreases. But as other resources get more investment, so must people. Employees are assets, not expenses. Consider Japan, where government, industry, and academia cooperate to improve their only natural resource, people.

Scherkenbach's observation about American education must be heeded to give the Deming way a chance of success in our educational system. "Industry desperately needs to foster teamwork. (But) teamwork in the classroom is called cheating . . . we need to develop teambuilding skills in our young people" (p.128). Cornesky takes it a step further with his view that education and self-improvement programs will succeed only with proper evaluations, recognition of weaknesses, and removal of fear from the system.

13.   End the Practice of Awarding Business on Pricetag

"End the practice of awarding business on the basis of price tag. Instead, minimize total cost. Move toward a single supplier for any one item on a long-term relationship of loyalty and trust" (Scherkenbach, 1988, p.131).

Meeting customers' needs at acceptable prices requires establishing long-term relationships with suppliers; only then are providers investing in continual improvement. This viewpoint is clearly applicable to postsecondary educational institutions. Faculty and administration must work closely with the school districts from which they recruit most of their students.

14.   Put Everybody to Work to Accomplish the Transformation

"Put everybody in the organization to work to accomplish the transformation. The transformation is everybody's job" (Scherkenbach, 1988, p.137).

We almost come full circle. Point five criticized common appraisal methods as barriers to continual improvement because they destroy teamwork. "The key to getting everyone involved in the transformation is to change the emphasis from individual performance reviews to systems evaluations" (Cornesky, 1989, p.149). Top management cannot delegate the responsibility because subordinates are likely to focus only on outcomes, not on processes which produce them. During the changeover management must work directly with the people in the process. Everyone must be willing to learn.

As the Deming way is implemented, a level of quality plateau is sometimes reached because "management (does) not (live) up to their responsibilities to change the processes that they are responsible for" (Scherkenbach, 1988, p.140). A three-pronged approach can prevent plateauing. Everyone in and directly related to the organization must be trained in ways which yield continual improvement. Management systems which inhibit continuing improvement must be rectified or removed. Opportunities to improve at every level must be identified and acted upon.

CAUTION

Having in mind a basic cognizance of Deming's philosophy and methods, the yellow caution flag should be raised. Members of the service sector, including educators, might be ready to "write off" Deming as too statistical; this may be especially true of many adult and continuing education specialists. However, let us critique his emphasis on statistics.

Deming powerfully advocates statistics as the language that managers and workers must share in order to learn which parts of the problems are caused by people and which by the system. Given the common aversion to applying hard data methods to the soft data business of adult and continuing education, the assumption can be quickly made that the Deming way requires only sophisticated statistics. Not true! The level of sophistication depends on the complexity of the system and the definition of quality. Deming's explanation of statistical tools, in his point about instituting modern methods of training, offers techniques that can be applied with varying levels of sophistication to meet the needs of different settings.

The emphasis on statistics increases rather than diminishes the role of workers. In fact, two of Deming's points, eliminate numerical goals and quantitative work standards, are based on the assertion that employees are not solely responsible for outcomes. Training, knowledge of the process, and tools and methods to operate the system must be substituted so that people work smarter toward constant improvement.

Be cautious while considering the applicability of Deming. "Students are not products, and professors do not work on a production line. But the mind set behind 'strategic quality management' offers useful templates for rethinking our commitments to quality and how we organize to achieve it" (Seymour, 1989, p.4). The comments of Daniel Seymour, visiting scholar in the Higher Education Institute at UCLA in 1989, point out key considerations for the application of corporate quality lessons to education and service organizations. He sees the focus on improving quality as a high-visibility organizational goal, a cultural transformation.

CONCLUSION

Applying the Deming way in continuing education and service organizations challenges us and requires commitment. But remember the distillation of Deming's philosophy and methodology: The pervasive concern related to improving quality is fulfilling management's responsibility to exercise leadership for the comprehensive and constant improvement of the system plus the on-going development of people as individuals and teammates.

In Chapter Two, Fendt integrates Deming's business viewpoint and Knowles' adult education perspective by showing that their top priority is the growth of people. Regardless of inputs, processes, and outcomes, organizations are people businesses. The leader's job is to enable people to improve through growth.

The application of the Deming way in specific organizational contexts is the theme of Chapters Three through Eight. From Cavaliere's macro-view of the massive land-grant university to Halverson's micro-look at classroom issues, from Tollett's work in a public school system to Cameron's discovery of many examples of quality advancement, the question is the same: What can be learned from Deming that will enable the systematic improvement of quality?

REFERENCES

Castro, Janice. "Making It Better" Time, November 13, 1989. New York, NY: The Time Magazine Co.

Cornesky, Robert A., et al. Deming: New Directions and Improving Quality, Public Acceptance and Competitive Positioning in Colleges and Universities. Edinboro University, Edinboro, PA 1989.

Deming, W. Edwards. Elementary Principles of the Statistical Control of Quality. Nippan Kagaku Gijutsu Remmei JUSE, 1951.

Deming, W. Edwards. Quality, Productivity, and Competitive Positioning and Out of the Crisis. Cambridge, MA: MIT Center for Advanced Engineering Study, 1986.

Dill, William R. "Management Education, Is Success Breeding Failure?", Change, March/April, 1989. Washington, DC: Heldref Publications.

Garvin, David A. "What Does 'Product Quality' Really Mean?", The Sloan Management Review, Fall 1984, p. 25-43.

Imai, Masaaki. Random House Business Division, New York.

Ishikawa, Kaoru. Guide to Quality Control. UNIPUB, 1983.

Kouzes, James M. and Posner, Barry Z. The Leadership Challenge--How to Get Extraordinary Things Done in Organizations. San Francisco, CA: Jossey-Bass, 1987.

QIP, Inc. Transformation of American Industry Training System. 1984.

Scherkenbach, William W. The Deming Route to Quality and Productivity - Road Maps and Roadblocks. Mercury Press/Fairchild Publications, Rockville, MD, 1988.

Seymour, Daniel, "Managing Quality in Higher Education," AAHE Bulletin, April, 1989, American Association for Higher Education, Washington, DC.

"Bringing Colleges Under Fire," Time, October 29, 1984. New York, NY: The Time Magazine Co.

Western Electric. Statistical Quality Control Handbook. 1954.

Wood, Robert Chapman. "A lesson learned and a lesson forgotten," Forbes, February 6, 1989. New York, NY: Forbes Inc.

CHAPTER TWO

COMPARING PHILOSOPHIES OF DEMING AND KNOWLES
Paul F. Fendt

When comparing two well known "fathers of significant movements," one from business and industry, the other from adult education, we find striking commonalities. Although their work was conceived apart and for different audiences, both Deming and Knowles sound the same notes with mature learners.

This chapter provides an overview of the philosophy behind the work of W. Edwards Deming, comparing and contrasting that philosophy with the adult education philosophy as expressed by Malcolm S. Knowles and several other authors of adult education literature.

Specifically, this chapter addresses two questions: (1) Are the applications of the philosophy of Deming consistent with the applications of the philosophy of adult education? and (2) Can the Deming philosophy assist in the management of programs for adult learners known as continuing education programs?

Since a point-by-point comparison between Knowles' adult education philosophy and the Deming philosophy is not apt to produce useful results, we shall describe the many parallels of behavioral and psychological intent which suggest that Deming applications in the MANAGEMENT of adult education programs do have merit.

According to Elias and Merriam, ". . . philosophy will be clarified by practice . . . " (1984, p. 8). In order to create a more graphic picture of Deming's philosophy vs. the philosophy of adult education, these assumptions are made: (1) Deming's "condensation of the 14 Points for Management" (Scherkenbach, 1988) constitutes the essence of the Deming philosophy; (2) Knowles' representation of adult education as a field of study, in his numerous publications, but specifically his Andragogical Model of HRD represents a viable philosophy of adult education for comparison (Knowles, 1990, pp. 118-120); and (3) the comparison of some philosophic assumptions about adults as managers of industrial workers (Deming) with some philosophic assumptions about adults as managers of the teaching/learning process (Knowles) can be enlightening in an initial determination of Deming's use to adult educators as managers of continuing education programs (Deming, 1989, pp. 23-24).

DEMING PHILOSOPHY

To form a basis for an applied adult education philosophy of Deming, his ". . . Fourteen Obligations of Top Management" in Chapter One cited by Vavrek will be our frame of reference.   A critique of the Deming philosophy will be found in Chapter Nine by Dew.

ADULT EDUCATION PHILOSOPHY

To form a selected basis for an applied adult education philosophy, we will use Knowles' andragogical model of human resource development as described in the book The Adult Learner: A Neglected Species (1990). Although Knowles does not represent the philosophy of adult education alone (such authors as Elias, Merriam and others have also made significant contributions), Knowles' concept of the andragogical model of human resource development is true to the tradition of adult education and best corresponds to our purposes. According to Knowles, "The andragogical teacher (facilitator, consultant, change agent) prepares in advance a set of procedures for involving the learners (and other relevant parties) in a process involving these elements:

1. Establishing a climate conducive to learning.
2. Creating a mechanism for mutual planning.
3. Diagnosing the needs for learning.
4. Formulating program/content objectives that will satisfy these needs.
5. Designing a pattern of learning experiences.
6. Conducting these learning experiences with suitable techniques and materials.

7.   Evaluating the learning outcomes and rediagnosing learning needs "
(Knowles, p. 120).

CRITIQUE OF KNOWLES PHILOSOPHY

To guide the comparison of the philosophies of Deming and Knowles, some critique of each is considered useful. The Knowles critique could be summarized as: "Andragogy has caused more controversy, philosophical debate, and critical analysis than any other concept/theory/model proposed thus far" (Merriam, 1987). Knowles' theory of how adults learn (andragogy) was a very much needed addition to learning theory for adults but critics agree that it may not be a "good fit" for every adult learner or for every learning situation.

Critics of Knowles' theory of andragogy challenged it as an organizing principle in adult education (Houle, 1972). Houle believed education was a single process or what Kidd calls "the seamless robe of learning" (Carlson, 1989). Again, Houle perceived andragogy as a technique, set of techniques or "that it is neither uniquely suited to adults nor superior to more traditional education" (Cross, 1981). In summary, according to Cross, "There is the question of whether andragogy is a learning theory (Knowles), a philosophical position (McKenzie), a political reality (Carlson), or a set of hypotheses subject to scientific verification (Elias)."

More recently, Merriam writes that "andragogy has caused more controversy, philosophical debate, and critical analysis than any other concept/theory/model..." (Merriam, 1987). An excellent 1988 article in Training magazine (Feuer and Gaber) cites the above by Merriam and summarizes some of the more contemporary critics of Knowles' self-directed learning, such as Brookfield who questioned whether self-directedness actually describes the typical adult learner or as Merriam concludes prescribes a goal for adult educators.

Most authors do concede that Knowles theories have had a major impact and have made a significant contribution to knowledge and understanding of adult learning issues. Merriam as quoted in Training by Feuer and Geber, regards Knowles as having "done enormous service to the field by creating a greater sensitivity among adult educators to the needs and interests of the learner."

Knowles and Deming may have the same basic fault: that their theories do not fit everyone or each situation. There are always exceptions, some of them major. Both authors devised theories to fit cases under their study and in their enthusiasm have overlooked many of the exceptions. Some authors say they were simply wrong but most agree to the enormous contribution to adult learning (Knowles) and to quality in management (Deming).

COMPARING DEMING AND KNOWLES

Concerning the crisis in American management, Deming states, "Transformation of American style of management is not a job of reconstruction, nor is it revision. It requires a whole new structure, from foundation upward" (Deming, p. ix). Similarly, with regard to the need for major educational change, Knowles writes, "Considering that the education of adults has been a concern of the human race for a very long time, it is curious that there has been so little thinking, investigating, and writing about adult learning until recently" (Knowles, p. 27).

Each author sees his contribution to knowledge as unique, as essential and as a radical departure from previous theory and practice. As Deming relates his 14 points as the philosophical basis for needed changes in management, he realizes that his is introducing a new way to American industry. Deming knows that managers must change their operating philosophy, their way of thinking about people and how people should work. Knowles also displays this sense of mission and destiny for education, specifically the education of the adult.

What then is the overlap between Deming and Knowles which would allow us to conclude that managers of adult learning programs would benefit from a study of Deming? The overlap incorporates many practical elements; it is not that both authors introduced a new era, although each did, but that both believed certain things about the way human beings must be treated in order to enable them to realize their potential as workers or as learners.

For Deming, people are what energizes the production system. The industrial system is more than machinery and data processing it is the people involved. ". . . few people in industry know what constitutes a system. . . . Few of them know that recruitment, training, supervision, and aids to production workers are part of the system" (Deming, p. 366). Deming cites examples of people with production problems. He goes into detail about the problem and then says, "It had never occurred to him that his people are part of the system. . ." (Deming, p. 368).

In a complimentary argument, Knowles asks, "How do you get people to be self-directed learners" (Knowles, 1989, p. 89)? Much of the energy of Knowles' career was devoted to helping learners become self-directed. "Always before they have been told by someone else - a teacher or trainer - what they are going to learn, how they are going to learn it, and whether they have learned it" (Knowles,   p. 89).

In these contexts of industry (production) and education (learning), Deming and Knowles have much in common, much to share with each other and we have much to benefit from such a comparison. Deming recognizes that it is people who make his system work and Knowles adds, yes, and let me show you how to make your production workers intelligent decision-makers and on-the-job thinkers. Make them self-directed in their learning about your company and its systems and hourly workers will perform like effective managers. Deming may agree with a flash of understanding in his eye, saying, yes "When he reaches it (statistical control), continuation of training by the same method will accomplish nothing" (Deming, p. 249). Knowles, says Deming, I can see where your self-directed learning would be beneficial for the production worker in statistical control, he can now help design his own training to a higher level of performance.

COMPARISONS AND CONTRASTS

As this chapter was being written, the Commission of Professors of Adult Education (of The American Association for Adult and Continuing Education) circulated their "Standards for Graduate Programs in Adult Education (February 1990)." Of immediate interest in relation to our comparison of philosophies were the following words:

> "Rationale for Standards - A concern for quality must dominate the planning, conduct, and evaluation of graduate programs in adult education. This concern is reflected in such outcomes as the preparation of adult educators with needed competencies and with a commitment to lifelong learning . . . and their contributions therein to leadership . . . . It is axiomatic that high quality   outcomes result from a combination of high quality input and processes. . . . processes are those forces, such as communication patterns, that operate within an organization to give it its dynamic nature" (Niemi, nd, p. 1).

This philosophy statement stands as an appropriate tribute to Knowles (and others) in realizing their earlier dreams for our professional field of adult education.

Just as a concern for quality headlines the standards for graduate programs, so quality concerns reach the heart of the matter for Deming, who asks, "What is the quality of a textbook, or of any book that its authors intended to carry a message of some kind" (Deming, p. 170)? Again Deming asks, "What is the quality of educational videotapes? Is it the photography that customers appreciate, or content" (Deming, p. 170)? "How do you define quality of teaching?" Deming continues: "How do you define a good teacher? . . . The only operational definition of knowledge requisite for teaching is research . . . . Publication of original research in reputable journals is an index of achievement. This is an imperfect measure, but none better has been found . . . . Why did people come from all over the world to study with them (teachers rated poor by some standards), including me? For the simple reason that these men had something to teach. They inspired their students . . . they were leaders of thought . . . . Their works will remain classic for centuries" (Deming, p. 173). For Deming and Knowles, quality in whatever one is doing is a continuous, lifelong process.

One other comparison occurs between Deming's workers who are in statistical control and Knowles' learning contract for the adult learner. For Knowles, it is "Without question the single most potent tool I have come across . . . . It has solved more problems that plagued me during my first forty years than any other invention. It provides . . . a way for individuals (and subgroups) to tailor-make their own learning plans. It solves the problem of getting the learner to have a sense of ownership of the objectives . . . " (Knowles, p. 139). Again Knowles says, "I now use learning contracts in all of may academic courses and in the in-service education programs in educational institutions, industry, and the professions in which I am a Consultant" (Knowles, p. 140).

For Deming it is statistical methods that are used to monitor training and to determine when it is completed. Statistical control is also an evaluation method which we shall discuss in greater detail.

In the context of quality, statistical control is the cue to suggest when training has been completed (is in a state of statistical control) and when additional training may be needed to move from one level or state of statistical control to another. For Deming, stable statistical control has advantages:

1. The process has an identity; its performance is predictable . . .
2. Costs are predictable.
3. Regularity of output is an important by-product of statistical control.
4. Productivity is at a maximum (costs at a minimum) under the present system.
5. Relationships with the vendor . . . are greatly simplified. Costs diminish as quality improves.
6. The effects of changes in the system . . . can be measured with greater speed and reliability . . .
7. The all-or-none rules (inspect all items or none) apply for minimum total cost of incoming items . . . (Deming, pp. 340 - 341).

COMPARING KNOWLES AND DEMING

According to Knowles' process elements, the andragogical teacher:

1. Establishes a climate conducive to learning.

In the <u>Deming Guide to Quality and Competitive Position</u> by Gitlow and Gitlow, the following observations are made: "Large organizations must begin to view themselves as families. Successful families endure and meet the physical and emotional needs of their members . . . . Their members are united around common goals and are committed to each other" (Gitlow and Gitlow, 1987, p. 15).

This description by the Gitlows would fit Knowles' concept of establishing a climate for learning. Knowles' operational definition of how this climate may be realized includes moving <u>from</u> a climate which is authority-oriented, formal and competitive (pedagogy - the old) <u>to</u> a climate of mutuality, respect, collaboration and informality (andragogy - the new) (Knowles, p. 119).

2. Creates a mechanism for mutual planning.

For Deming, this concept may best parallel his use of charts showing whether the worker is in statistical control. Deming's point 14 (Put everybody in the organization to work to accomplish the transformation. The transformation is everybody's job . . .) (Scherkenbach, p. 137) indicates that everyone knows what the objectives are and when they have been achieved. Deming recommends that employees know when they have achieved the desired outcome by measures of statistical control. Deming writes, "Sound understanding of statistical control is essential to management, engineering, manufacturing, purchase of materials, and service" (Deming, p. 322). A number of charts, graphs and other visual methods based upon simple statistics tell the worker when (s)he is in statistical control.

For Knowles, planning is the "one aspect of educational practice that most sharply differentiates the pedagogical from the andragogical, the mechanistic from the organistic, and the 'teaching' from the 'facilitating of learning' schools of thought . . . " (Knowles, p. 125).

As Deming recommends that all levels of the organization become involved in adopting the new organizational philosophy (Deming point 2), so Knowles believes " . . . that a cardinal principle of andragogy . . . is that a mechanism must be provided for involving all parties concerned in the educational enterprise in its planning" (Knowles, p. 125).

    3.   Diagnoses the needs for learning.

According to Knowles, "It is not assumed that the learner necessarily starts out contributing his perceptions to the model; he may not know the requisite abilities of a new situation" (Knowles, p. 127). In this section of his book, Dr. Knowles discusses the building of a model for diagnosing the learner's needs, asserting that "There are three sources of data for building such a model: the individual, the organization, and the society" (Knowles, p. 126). Knowles talks about developing operational statements or competencies and how the human resources developer may expose the learner to role models so that (s)he can begin to develop a realistic model individually. "Organizational perceptions of desired performance are obtained through systems analysis, performance analyses (Mager 1972), and analyses of . . . job descriptions, safety reports, productivity records, supervisors' reports, personnel appraisals, and cost/effectiveness studies" (Knowles, p. 127). Finally, Knowles discusses discrepancies between where the learner is now and where (s)he wants to be. This is essentially a self-assessment for the learner, guided by the organization and the society in which this organization functions.

Perhaps an even better philosophical fit between Deming's philosophy and adult education philosophy is the concept of "Staged Self-Directed Learning" by Grow (1990). His model matches the maturity level of the adult learner with the appropriate kind of teacher response:

STAGED SELF-DIRECTED LEARNING MODEL (Grow, p. 2)

The teacher's purpose is to match the learner's stage of self-direction and prepare the learner to advance to higher stages.

STAGE	STUDENT	TEACHER	EXAMPLES
Stage 1	Dependent	Authority	Coaching with immediate feedback. Drill. Informational lecture. Overcoming deficiencies and resistance.
Stage 2	Interested	Motivator, guide	Inspiring lectures plus guided discussion. Goal-setting and learning strategies.
Stage 3	Involved	Facilitator	Discussion facilitated by teacher who participates as equal. Seminar. Group projects.
Stage 4	Self-Directed	Consultant, delegator	Internship, Dissertation, individual work or self-directed study-group

Like Grow, Deming is concerned with what the worker knows and what (s)he can be expected to know. "People learn in different ways. Some have difficulty to learn by written instructions (dyslexia). Others have difficulty to learn by the spoken word (dysphasia). Some people learn best by pictures; others by imitation; some by a combination of methods" (Deming, p. 52). According to Knowles, Grow, and Deming, the new paradigm is an essential way to share with the adult learner (Knowles and Grow) or worker (Deming) what the new philosophy is, how it can be accessed, and how it will help individuals to reach their goals and production in life.

For Deming, one model for implementing the new philosophy is the Shewhart cycle (in Japan it is called the Deming cycle), developed by Walter A. Shewhart, Graduate School, Department of Agriculture, Washington, D. C., 1939.

The Shewhart/Deming cycle " . . . is a procedure to follow for improvement of any stage; also a procedure for finding a special cause detected by statistical signal" (Deming, p. 88).

The first stage of the cycle is planning for a change. Next you carry out the change, preferably on a small scale. Then the results are checked and we ask ourselves what we learned? Finally, and most importantly, we act: adopt the change, abandon the change or run through it again, possibly under different environmental conditions.

Clearly Knowles could "live with" this approach; actually, the cycle is very close to Knowles' program evaluation model, in which evaluation leads back to new planning or new changes for later evaluation. Although we do not have an exact "fit" here between Knowles and Deming, their respective philosophies seem compatible and instructive, one to the other.

4.   Formulates Program Objectives (content) that will satisfy these needs.

"Adult education theorists have tended to build design models into which aspects [of other] approaches can be fitted. The three most recent are by Knowles, Tough and Houle (in order of publication). The andragogical design model involves choosing problem areas that have been identified by the learners through self-diagnostic procedures and selecting appropriate formats (individual, group, and mass activities) for learning . . . " (Knowles, p. 133). Knowles then describes how Houle expands his model to encompass the individual, the group, the institution, and a mass audience. Part of Knowles' point is to stress self-directed learning, with which Deming deals only indirectly.

Deming does spend a number of pages in Out of the Crisis on operational definitions. Here he is suggesting that, in order to know what programs or work objectives we are working toward, we should define them operationally so that we know when we have reached them and so that everyone is "speaking the same language" or referring to the same event.

5. and 6.   Operates the program and then evaluates the learning outcomes.

At this point Knowles establishes a series of steps in the evaluation process:

a.   Reaction evaluation - This is otherwise known as formative evaluation, or "getting data about how the participants are responding to a program as it takes place . . ." (Knowles, p. 137).

b.   Learning evaluation - getting data about the principles, facts, and techniques which were acquired by the participants.

c.   Behavior evaluation - requiring data such as observers' reports about actual changes in what the learner does after the training as compared with what (s)he did before.

d.   Results evaluation - data which are usually contained in the routine records of an organization - including effects on turnover, costs, efficiency, frequency of accidents, grievances or tardiness or absences, quality control rejections, and the like" (Knowles, p. 137).

Both Deming and Knowles agree that improvement must be constant and ongoing. A section of Deming's book deals with constancy of purpose. By this he appears to mean that the worker and management strive to constantly improve their product, their operations, and their work atmosphere so that there is a tomorrow. Deming asks, "Who will survive? Companies that adopt constancy of purpose for quality, productivity, and service, and go about it with intelligence and perseverance, have a chance to survive" (Deming, p. 155). For Deming the evaluation process is centered around statistical control. When a worker is not in statistical control, training can help move that person toward statistical control, toward a more predictable level of performance. When the employee reaches a level of statistical control, no more training of this type will move him or her to higher levels. At this point a new training program must be devised to achieve higher levels of quality.

Again, Deming would share many methods with Knowles. One of these is brainstorming. Some of Deming's statistical recommended processes aid in the constant attempt to improve the overall quality of the enterprise. Flow charts, check sheets, Pareto analysis (separating the most important characteristics of an event from the least important in graphic form), fishbone diagram (indicating complex relationships - somewhat akin to a sociogram for example, in a social context), histogram, and scatter diagrams (frequency of events on an X and Y axis with a line drawn where there is a strong positive or negative correlation) are some of Demings' statistical recommended processes.

CAN CONTINUING EDUCATION ORGANIZATIONS BENEFIT FROM DEMING'S PHILOSOPHY?

In this author's opinion, Deming and Knowles (representing adult education) have much in common. They both desired to make a major impact upon what they believed was wrong. For Deming, it was a misguided set of management practices leading America to industrial mediocrity. For Knowles, it was an uninformed set of educational practices which totally ignored what was unique about adults and how they learn so that most adults felt out-of-place in the formal learning environments of education. The work of these two pioneers is still underappreciated and under-utilized, but that is changing.

"The beginning of wisdom is this: Get Wisdom and whatever you get, get insight" (Psalm 4:7).

"Keep hold of instruction, do not let go; guard her, for she is your life" (Psalm 4:13).

REFERENCES

Carlson, Robert A. "Malcolm Knowles: Apostle of Andragogy, "Vitae Scholasticae. Volume 8, No. 1, 1989.

Cross, K. Patricia. Adults as Learners: Increasing Participation and Facilitating Learning. San Francisco: Jossey-Bass, 1981.

Deming, W. E. Out of the Crisis. Cambridge, Massachusetts: MIT Center for Advanced Engineering Study, 1989.

Elias, J. and Merriam, S. Philosophical Foundations of Adult Education. Malabar, Florida: Robert E. Krieger Publishing Company, 1984.

Feuer, D. and B. Geber. "Uh-Oh...Second Thoughts about Adult Learning Theory." Training. December 1988.

Gitlow, H. and Gitlow, S. The Deming Guide to Quality and Competitive Position. Englewood Cliffs, New Jersey: Prentice- Hall, Inc., 1987. Houston, Texas: Gulf Publishing Company, 1978.

Grow, G. "Staged Self-Directed Learning." A paper presented to the Conference on Adult Self-Directed Learning, University of Oklahoma, February 1990.

Houle, Cyril O. The Design of Education. San Francisco: Jossey-Bass, 1972.

Knowles, M. The Adult Learner: A Neglected Species. Houston, Texas: Gulf Publishing Company, Fourth Edition, 1990. The Making of an Adult Educator: An Autobiographical Journey. San Francisco: Jossey-Bass, Inc. 1989.

Merriam, Sharan. Adult Education Quarterly. Washington, D. C.: American Association for Adult and Continuing Education, Summer 1987.

Niemi, John A. February 28, 1990 letter from Professor Niemi with flier attached. "Standards for Graduate Programs in Adult Education, "Commission of Professors of Adult Education of the American Association for Adult and Continuing Education (no date).

Scherkenbach, W. The Deming Route to Quality and Productivity: Road Maps and Road Blocks. Washington, DC: Ceep Press, 1988.

CHAPTER THREE

LAND-GRANT UNIVERSITIES AND QUALITY IMPROVEMENT
Lorraine A. Cavaliere

Deming provides processes for land-grant institutions to adopt a new quality philosophy as a means to deliver improved products and services to many diverse constituents of the complex organization.

Organizations are complex structures composed of people and resources. Service organizations systematize these people and resources into a variety of production modes to deliver a service product to a specified clientele. Land-grant institutions are service organizations charged with the mission to educate students through research, teaching and public service. How can these institutions of education improve the quality of their service? This chapter compares and analyzes characteristics of land-grant institutions and Deming's management method. The analyses offer a framework to critique methodological applications of Deming's management principles as a means to improve the quality of products and services provided by these institutions.

A service organization must undertake the following tasks to work effectively with the clients: determine target clients, identify their needs, develop services that match needs, make the services available, and communicate these services to the target clients (Kotler, 1975, p.32). The students are the clients receiving the services of the educational organization, for which they pay fees. These fees rarely cover the costs of providing the services and the deficit must be made up by raising money from donors and the government. Land-grant institutions are essentially this type of service organization.

The complexities of organizations often interfere with the ability to determine their effectiveness. Therefore, the delineation of the concept and characteristics of an organization provides a framework for analyses of organizational systems. The concept of the organization can be elucidated through an analogy:

The Red Wheelbarrow

So much depends

upon

a red wheel

barrow

glazed with rain

water

beside the white

chickens.

William Carlos Williams (1883-1963)

(Abcarian, 1972, p.75)

The wheelbarrow is to the chickens as the educational institution is to the students, is the service mechanism of the organization. It provides the structural framework to deliver the support services to the clients. The wheelbarrow must be made of highly durable parts. And the person handling the wheelbarrow must use it efficiently for the system to be maintained. If the components of the organization (wheelbarrow, persons and resources) maintain high quality in the delivery of their services, the chickens go on to produce items and services to support society. If the service organization becomes faulty and fails to provide service of the highest quality, the chickens (clients) are immediately affected and stop producing the same volume of eggs; subsequently less chickens are reproduced. Their production dwindles; their numbers lessen; their service to the larger society is diminished. The entire organization is deemed useless.

These same principles apply to institutions of education as service organizations. The wheelbarrow is the same as the structural and support mechanisms of the university, i.e. administrative structure, buildings, grounds, food, etc. The people operating the wheelbarrow are the faculty and staff of the organization and the students are those serviced, the clients. Quality services provided to the students produce a highly educated individual adequately equipped to interact with and contribute to the larger society. If the organization is not of the highest quality, the students cannot learn and achieve to their highest potential. Thus, they receive a less than adequate education, which in turn makes them inferior competitors for employment. This chain of events directly impacts the economic competitiveness of the country in the world market. If the educational institution provides the highest quality service to its clients, everyone benefits from the quality service.

Deming's 14-point program, for the most part, has been successfully implemented in business and industry. This chapter explores the nature of land-grant institutions as service organizations and how Deming's methods may serve as process indicators to revamp traditional educational institutions from archaic bureaucracies to high quality, service-oriented delivery mechanisms.

LAND-GRANT INSTITUTIONS: CONCEPTS AND CONTRIBUTIONS

Land-grant institutions constitute a major vehicle for postsecondary education in the United States. Their evolution during the decades following the Civil War transformed American higher education. During those post war years colleges and universities placed increased emphasis on science and practical subjects while refocusing the curricula towards the needs of society. Economic, political, and social forces moved higher education from classicism to secularism. The demand for more technical and scientific training to benefit farmers and industrial workers spurred Congress to enact legislation that would revolutionize the institution of higher education.

Justin Morrill, a congressional representative of Vermont, authored the Morrill Land Grant College Act of 1862 and 1890. These provided land to states to support universities whose mission was to teach subjects related to agriculture and the mechanical arts. Subsequent legislation that forged the concept of the land-grant institution were the Hatch Act of 1887 and the Smith-Lever Act of 1914. These laws, combined with the Morrill Acts, crystallized a national system of education that now combined classical studies with courses in science, agriculture, and mechanical arts.

Expanded curricula and related research were now, by law, bridged to society through experiment stations and extension services. The basic concepts of this land-grant model, as forged by Congress, provided for the democratization of education, the conduct of applied research to benefit the people of the states, and service rendered directly to the citizenry through extension agents, short courses, and continuing education. (Anderson, 1976, p.1). As the twentieth century dawned, other public and private institutions adapted and incorporated the basic concepts of the land-grant model so that now little distinction exists among public postsecondary institutions.

The contributions of land-grant institutions have had a profound effect on the discovery and dissemination of knowledge. The legislation that forged the land-grant model, and the adoption of land-grant concepts by many other postsecondary institutions, established a mechanism that could provide education to diverse populations with comprehensive curricula offerings reflective of the needs of a democratic society. This unique partnership of nation and state brought about an expansion of educational opportunity through the democratization of higher education. Individuals from diverse economic, racial, ethnic, and gender groups had access to higher education.

This new philosophy for higher education forged by legislation brought many more educational opportunities to the citizenry. It provided a combination of vocational education and liberal arts education. The formation of the agricultural experiment stations were a direct result of the infusion of agriculture and the mechanic arts in the organizational and research missions of the institution. Through the university extension divisions and the cooperative extension service, research is disseminated to people, business, and industry, allowing education to be a continuing process. The land-grant model called for military training and leadership which led to the formation of the Reserve Officer Training Corps (ROTC).

Above all, the land-grant system provides an exemplary and effective model for combining federal and state funds to finance higher education. As Jones, Oberst and Lewis (1990, p.12) suggest, "this model . . . offers a possible solution for how to improve America's industrial strength tomorrow through the creation of a public infrastructure for American engineering and technology."

THE UTILITY OF THE DEMING WAY

The historical evolution of land-grant institutions provides a rational context from which to analyze the mission and service of the present day institution. The dramatic increases in enrollments since World War II raises the question as to whether these institutions provide mechanisms to ensure quality to quantity. "It must not be forgotten that Justin Morrill's vision was not just that there should be equality of opportunity for higher education, but that this education should be quality education" (Anderson, 1976, p.18). Deming offers a quality improvement model to examine and incorporate in the operation of an organization to this end. The analysis of this functional management method relative to the characteristics of land-grant institutions offers an opportunity to explore the potential for quality improvement.

Since many land-grant institutions can be generally characterized as slow-to-change bureaucracies, what can be done to make them more responsive to their clients and constituents while offering quality products and services? Deming offers 14 points which have proven successful in fulfilling this goal and which can serve as a framework to analyze its utility within the land-grant institution. Some questions that guide the analysis are: What aspects of the organization are especially receptive or resistant to the Deming way? How might the receptivity and resistance become managerial guideposts? Which of Deming's points are highly applicable or not so to which organizational characteristics (and why)? How would the focus on quality affect the people within the organization? What would be the short and long-term changes in the reward system that supports the dedication to quality? What implications for change does the practice of Deming's method have on these organizations?

1: Create constancy of purpose toward improvement of product and service, with the aim to become competitive, stay in business, and provide jobs.

Constancy of purpose is manifested through the mission statement and goals of the organization. Does the institution have a mission statement? If so, is it clearly articulated and disseminated so that the institutional community is not only aware of the statements but has internalized the concepts that in turn translate as behavioral guideposts? The mission statement provides a fundamental view of the basic character of the institution. This view gains constancy toward improvement of product and service through planning, research, and innovation. Strategic planning, involving all who are impacted, is a critical process that needs to be fluid, continuous, and evolutionary. The research involves understanding the needs of the customer through constant statistical market research and customer feedback. Environmental scanning of contextual external forces informs the strategic planning process and leads to innovation without fear of failure. This combination of planning, research, and innovation leads to the development of highly specific action plans and resource allocation decisions logically ensue. These processes should all be employed to better serve the user groups of the organization, i.e. students, staff, faculty, and other publics. Deming's initial point provides specific processes to focus and improve the organization to provide the highest quality education available to the students. It involves rigorous planning and staff involvement practices that must be implemented by top management.

2: Adopt the new philosophy. We are in a new economic age. Western management must awaken to the challenge, must learn their responsibilities, and take on leadership for change.

Deming's philosophy posits that higher quality costs less, not more, This is the philosophy of the new economic age. Higher quality is achieved by improving the processes of the organization; and productivity increases as quality improves. This is a direct result of less "rework" or as described in higher education: corrective behaviors also knows as repetitive and redundant work caused by errors and/or lack of information. When management focuses on improving the process to avoid "rework," the time spent on one task lessens while productivity and quality improve, (Scherkenbach, 1986, p.19). All the sub-systems within land-grant institutions could benefit from constant analysis of their service processes. Imaging how dining services, housing, registration, and transportation might be improved by systematically and continually examining and refining their performance and production processes to improve delivery of these services to the students. In adopting the new philosophy, the focus changes from competitive comparisons to customer satisfaction. This philosophical revolution can only occur when top management provides the leadership for this change.

All administration must clearly understand this new orientation toward customer service and quality products; clearly defined lines of communication must be designed and implemented to disseminate the new philosophy. Written and oral communiques need to be distributed and discussed, through consistent modes, throughout the organization. The new philosophy needs to be modeled by management and behavioral standards need to be clearly defined. As perspectives and attitudes change, a true sense of service and mission to the students results. From a management perspective this point is more easily stated than implemented. However, it is highly plausible and the end result if immediately rewarding.

3: Cease dependence on inspection to achieve quality. Eliminate the need for inspection on a mass basis by building quality into the product in the first place.

Analysis of the "inspection" systems within land-grant institutions surface procedures and policies rooted in strong historic and academic traditions: tenure, tests, final exams, performance evaluations, disciplinary actions, grievances, etc. All of these procedures are evaluation mechanisms employed "after the fact." Defects in performance and knowledge are supposedly detected at the outcome phase of the process. The student is accepted, takes the required course, then tested for competency. The student is sent on to higher level requirements if performance on the test is satisfactory. If failure occurs, the student is "scrapped or reworked" to use Deming's terminology. A more responsive and productive method would be constant evaluation of the process that the product (student) is flowing through. If the product is faulty, the system is faulty. Examination of recruiting techniques and evaluation measures, with the Deming perspective, could lead to improvements in the process that serves the product and thus the product would be improved.

Performance evaluations are attempts to evaluate behavior of staff after the fact. According to Deming, if the employee is performing inadequately, it is probably the fault of the system. Tenure also rewards a culmination of years of teaching and research or rejects from the system those who have not met terminal tenure requirements. A tremendous loss of talent, time, and hard work is the result of this rejection process for the individual and the institution. Do these present evaluation techniques guarantee quality of student, staff, and faculty performance? How can quality be insured without these evaluation techniques? Improve the process through continuous statistical observations and feedback of product (student, staff, faculty) development. The implementation of this point requires a complete reformation of the reward system inculcated in the educational systems that exist today. Every process from promotions to merit pay for faculty and staff as well as acceptance requirements to graduation for the student rests upon the present evaluation (inspection) methods. It requires strong leadership to revamp such a traditional system. This leadership requires the ability to incorporate the previous processes of planning, research and innovation coupled with a clear vision for change to being about these dramatic changes in the current institutionalized reward system.

4: End the practice of awarding business on the basis of price tag. Instead, minimize total cost. Move toward a single supplier for any one item on a long-term relationship of loyalty and trust.

Anyone having experience with government purchasing procedures will quickly realize the ramifications of this point. Within land-grant institutions there is usually a purchasing department through which all other departments must send requests for purchases (purchase orders) to obtain equipment and services. Any given individual does not have the authority to purchase items independently. The purchasing department adheres to policies, institutional and governmental, that regulate these purchasing processes. As a result, bidding and contract methods are employed to secure the cheapest price. However, often quality is either not considered or cannot be measured. In turn, the required equipment and services are inconsistent, impersonal, and very often inappropriate. Unlimited scenarios of inefficiency result for all involved. However, the system persists due to institutional policies and legislative requirements.

How can these be changed to bring about efficient purchase of and subsequent service for equipment and services? This is not easily answered, given the complexity of the relationships among the agencies involved. And the entire process must rely on trust and loyalty that needs to be fostered from central administration within the organization. This point would probably encounter high levels of resistance within the current infrastructures of land-grant institutions unless mandates ensued from state legislatures and boards of governors. Resistance to change on this point stems from historical patterns that evolved from dealing with a single supplier. Corruption, monopolies, and unions forced the formation of current purchasing practices and mandated changes for federal and state sources are necessary to jog the system into more efficient and productive service modes.

5:   Improve constantly and forever the system of production and service, to improve quality and productivity, and thus constantly decrease costs.

According to Deming, quality must be incorporated into every step of the production process beginning with the design stage. Within a service organization this translates to processes, programs, and policies upon which the organization operates. The initial design stages of academic programs and institutional policies and practices require a continuous review system to implement constant improvements in quality and productivity. This improvement system needs to involve everyone within the organization. Planning and review committees need to be established at all levels hierarchically as well as across disciplines to evaluate programs, processes and practices for effectiveness and revision.

The input and feedback from these committees must have the capability to impact policy changes and directly respond to student and societal needs. Again, central administration must implement and support these efforts and respond in kind. Currently the processes of external review and accreditation offer evaluation, suggestions for improvement, and sanctions. These are not, however, indigenous to the internal perspectives of the organization and therefore become evaluation standards to be tolerated and subsequently incorporated. When the improvement processes arise from vested sources, contextual and cultural forces inform the decision-making processes and changes are implemented with commitment.

6: Institute training on the job.

Staff development and training models currently employed usually reflect formats that are superimposed, sporadic, and out of the context of the work situation. Staff and faculty rarely experience professional development at the work station or in the classroom. These professional development activities lack uniformity and consistency. And since they are usually out of context, individual behavior is not changed in the workplace. A comprehensive, institution-wide professional development program that supports the goal of total quality management and quality service would provide coherence and focus. To offer these training opportunities within the context of the workplace and/or teaching and learning environment would enhance direct application of the newly acquired skills and provide meaningful learning experiences. In addition to the contact skills necessary to perform the job, Deming teaches that knowledge of statistical thinking

44

and application of statistical methods are necessary skills for all employees to learn on the job. Differentiated staffing models using mentors and tutors foster this type of contextual learning.

7: Institute leadership. The aim of leadership should be to help people, machines and gadgets to do a better job. Supervision of management is in need of overhaul, as well as supervision of production workers.

Within the bureaucracy of land-grant institutions, management is rarely equated with leadership. Bureaucracies reward status quo, while leadership requires vision, innovation, and action. In the United States this dichotomy is intensified because "within any organization, an entrenched bureaucracy with a commitment to the status quo undermines the unwary leader. To make matters worse, certain social forces--the increasing tension between individual rights and the common good . . . discourage the emergence of leaders" (Bennis, 1989, p. xii). Many experts have philosophized and researched the concept and qualities of leadership. There is little consensus on the definition of a leader and whether, in fact, leadership can be taught. However, people seem to recognize a leader when they see one.

Given the amorphous, yet identifiable, construct of leadership, how does an organization institute leadership? The top administration must set the tone by hiring and fostering individuals who are visionaries, change agents, courageous, value-driven, flexible and action-oriented; those who do not manage the status quo, but who effect continual improvements and change to provide quality products and service to their constituents (Tichy and Devanna, 1986). This approach requires altered reward systems for employees and perspective changes within the organization's culture. As Gardner suggests, "Perhaps what every (organization) needs is a Department of Continuous Renewal that would view the whole organization as a system in need of continuing innovation" (1981, p.76).

8: Drive out fear, so that everyone may work effectively for the company.

Fear is fueled by such current practices as "serve at the pleasure," unions, grievance procedures, tenure, merit pay, budget cuts, grant awards, performance evaluations, secrecy of top administration, and communication barriers. There is fear of not knowing and fear that other people will find out what you do know. In order for a management system to work that is based on the new philosophy, an atmosphere of mutual respect must exist. In their implementation of the Deming method, the School of Science, Management and Technologies at Edinboro University of Pennsylvania suggests that "administrators should attempt to drive out fear by establishing trust through positioning, confidence through respect, and meaning through communication" (Deal, 1989, p.85). This trust and confidence are achieved by administrators exhibiting consistent, persistent, and reliable behavior. In Scherkenbach's analysis of Deming's points, the possibility of eliminating fear altogether seems improbable. However, he suggests that this point should be the first one implemented to ensure quality management, since it affects the implementation of most all of the other points.

9: Break down barriers between departments. People in research, design, sales and production must work as a team to foresee problems in production and in use that may be encountered with the product or service.

To the educational institution this implicates all academic, administrative and support services to be actively involved in cross fertilizing information across department lines. This information comes in the form of feedback from customers as well as statistical data collected by each department about their processes. This information needs to be understood and shared in order to meet the needs of the customer, in this case, the students. As Scherkenbach states: "The obvious challenge is to get everyone involved in the innovation, everyone recognizing that they each have something to contribute and they can do so in an atmosphere of mutual respect . . . operationally defining the ultimate customers' needs and expectation so that everyone understands how he contributes to the success of the organization is a solid step toward breaking down barriers between departments" (p. 82). Once the mission and action plans have been articulated and disseminated, everyone in the organization needs to meet interdepartmentally to exchange information regularly about processes and customer service. The deans need to meet with other central administrators. The chairpersons need to meet with the deans. And cross-disciplinary meetings need to ensue with other administrative and support units. The more information and planning that is shared across department barriers, the more the individual will feel part of the process of making the organization a quality service system.

46

10: Eliminate slogans, exhortations, and targets for the work force that ask for zero defects and new levels of productivity.

All personnel within the organization must be trained to use statistical procedures to determine standard deviations in the quality of products and services. Only then can observations based on facts be used to determine changes needed to improve the production process. The system and its processes must be improved and stabilized by administrative leaders, not by slogans. Usually when problems arise within land-grant institutions, administration and affected factions of the organization develop slogans and themes that represent the actions designed to remedy the problems and effect change. The slogans and themes serve to move individuals and groups to action and rally support for their cause. However, these methods blur the focus of the change strategies and energy is expended on promoting the slogans and campaigns rather than getting the job done. Granted, there is a certain contagious atmosphere that spreads through inspirational slogans and quota campaigns. Fund raising contingents successfully use these techniques on a regular basis. Deming contends that true information based on observation and measurement about organizational processes should serve as the motivating force for employees and employers alike, rather than the shallow inspiration promoted through company slogans and quota campaigns.

11: Eliminate work standards (quotas) on the factory floor. Substitute leadership. Eliminate management by objective. Eliminate management by numbers, numerical goals. Substitute leadership.

As long as enrollment figures drive budget appropriations, the financial infrastructure of a land-grant institution will prioritize full-time enrollment (FTEs) statistics as a major numerical goal. Grants and external funding sources drive decision making as sure as the size of the endowment. Athletics brings higher rewards to those students involved than liberal arts due to the dollar figures attached to national athletic acclaim versus intellectual performance. The resource allocation system needs to be mutually planned by all parties involved, not based solely on enrollment figures. Administration must communicate plans with faculty to improve and provide services and facilities for faculty to be able to do the best possible teaching and research. Out of this collegial atmosphere of growth and quality, trust will be established and quotas will be unnecessary. All the quotas in the universe cannot improve production if the system is faulty.

12: Remove barriers that rob the hourly worker of his right to pride of workmanship. The responsibility of supervisors must be changed from stressing sheer numbers to quality. Remove barriers that rob people in management and engineering of that right to pride of workmanship. This means, inter alia, abolishment of the annual merit rating and of management by objective.

Most systems within land-grant institutions are unionized. The American Association of University Professors, the AFL-CIO and other representative labor unions control many of these practices through contractual agreements and bargaining agencies. These unions seem to confine and impede individual impetus by setting external standards of performance and parameters for job descriptions. Administrators are either hindered or intimidated by union contracts in building collegial and mutually defined plans for performance. Unions often protect the incompetent and hinder those with initiative. In addition, evaluation that is an outgrowth of union contracts, such as management by objectives and merit pay, fosters "short-term performance, annihilates long-term planning, builds fear, demolishes teamwork, nourishes rivalry and politics" (Deming, p.102). During the planning process, specifications for a range of outcomes should be determined, rather than specific attribute outcomes. Then the focus for evaluation shifts to the process and away from the individual. Statistical tracking of development stages of the product or service then informs the decision-making about where the processes can be improved and/or changed to improve quality. Should it be a reflection on the faculty if graduation statistics are low for the members of the football team or should be recruitment, retention, and instructional processes by analyzed? When the processes are scrutinized, the reasons for failure become clear and the system is implicated, not the people.

13: Institute a vigorous program of education and self-improvement.

A vigorous program of education and self-improvement needs to be pervasive and continuous throughout the organization. As computerization of routines occurred throughout higher education, a tremendous need for learning was felt by all who were required to use this new technology. This need for education and training was a direct result of innovation. With Deming's method in operation, continuous education and self-improvement would be a natural extension of constant improvements and adjustments to the organizational systems. For pervasive and continuous educational opportunities to occur within the organization, resources must be allocated to the academic departments and administrative offices of the university. These resource allocation decisions are a resultant variable of the planning processes as stated in Points 1 and 5 of Deming. The nature and topic of professional development activities, including travel, should be mutually decided by staff, faculty and administration while remaining consistent with the mission and goals of the organization. The allocation of resources for these types of activities needs to be equitable and reasonable. And this is not always easy to do within a large bureaucracy due to historical operating patterns and funding formulas. However, even when resources are limited, the spirit for lifelong learning can be contagious. The deans and department chairs can set the tone for this type of activity and involvement by having free lecture series, study circles, research sharing sessions, grant and fellowship activities, etc. Central administration needs to support these efforts through renovation of the institutional reward systems.

14: Put everybody in the organization to work to accomplish the transformation. The transformation is everybody's job.

This last point calls for the understanding, implementation and synthesis of the preceding 13 points by every member of the organization. For this to occur top management must organize as a team to comprehend and implement this quality method. A statistical methodology must be implemented, usually by a statistical consultant, to teach and implement analytical procedures to guide the quality improvement process. Training and dissemination strategies must be designed and implemented to school all employees in the precise idea of continual quality improvement. A reorientation of thinking and practice must occur to include a four-step cyclical and continuous process: 1. systems analyses to identify needed changes; 2. implementing the changes; 3. observing the effects of the changes; and 4. using the observations and related learning to begin the process all over again. Leadership and knowledge of the process are essential to the successful implementation of the Deming method.

CONCLUSION

Since change is deemed the only constant in life, can institutions of higher education afford not to consider Deming's principles as a method to improve the quality of their organizations and services? This quality management and performance could effect positive changes in related educational systems within our society. Administrators in higher education need to make a concerted effort to understand the principles and practices that ensure a quality education. This means intensive study and collaboration with colleagues to develop a philosophy of quality that constitutes a constancy of purpose. The resultant strategic planning would reflect societal trends of the future and focus on constant improvement of the systems of the organization, rather than on maintaining status quo. Administrators and faculty would then be working closely with their publics fulfilling their mission of providing a quality education. To what extent could the Deming method be operationalized within your organization?

50

REFERENCES

Abcarian, Richard, Words in Flight: An Introduction to Poetry. Belmont, California: Wadsworth Publishing Co., Inc., 1972.

Anderson, G. Lester (ed.). Land-Grant Universities and Their Continuing Challenge. Michigan: Michigan State University Press, 1976.

Bennis, Warren. Why Leaders Can't Lead: The Unconscious Conspiracy Continues. San Francisco: Jossey-Bass Publishers, 1989.

Deal, Elsie, (ed.). Deming: New Directions for Improving Quality, Public Acceptance and Competitive Positioning in Colleges and Universities. Edinboro University of Pennsylvania: School of Science, Management & Technologies, 1989.

Gardner, John W. Self-Renewal: The Individual and The Innovative Society. New York: W.W. Norton & Co., 1981.

Jones, Russel C., Oberst, Bethany A., and Lewis, Courtland S. "The Land Grant Model." Change, May/June, 1990, 11-17.

Kotler, Philip. Marketing for Nonprofit Organizations. Englewood Cliffs, New Jersey: Prentice-Hall, Inc., 1975.

McCormick, Richard P. Rutgers: A Bicentennial History. New Jersey: Rutgers University Press, 1966.

McDade, Sharon A. Higher Education Leadership: Enhancing Skills Through Professional Development Programs. ASHE-ERIC Higher Education Report No. 5. Washington, D.C.: Association for the Study of Higher Education, 1987.

Scherkenbach, William W. The Deming Route to Quality and Productivity. Washington, D.C.: CEEPress Books, 1987.

Tichy, Noel M. and Devanna, Mary Ann. "The Transformational Leader." Training and Development Journal. 1986, July, 27-32.

The Development of the Land-Grant Colleges and Universities and Their Influence on the Economic and Social Life of the People. Addresses given at a series of ten seminars sponsored by The College of Agriculture, Forestry, and Home Economics. West Virginia University, 1962.

CHAPTER FOUR

PRIVATE CONTINUING HIGHER EDUCATION AND DEMING: MATCH OR MISMATCH?

Jerome F.E. Halverson

Private continuing higher education seems to be more naturally compatible with Deming's principles but all systems resist change.

Continuing higher education and Deming are coming of age. The spirit of continuing higher education is nested in the land grant institutions tradition to blend research with practice; and in the liberal arts core of private institutions which was to be the foundation for life-long intellectual and spiritual growth and development.

Deming is a more recent and powerful reminder that continuous improvement is not merely a nifty slogan but an essential foundation for personal and corporate, public and private survival. The learning symbiosis created by merging continuing higher education and Deming is potentially transformative.

In this chapter I will focus on: a) characteristics of private institutions in general; and b) several of Deming's 14 obligations as they apply to private continuing higher education.

Though Deming developed 14 obligations, in this chapter I have chosen to comment on five which, in my opinion, serve as the foundation for the remaining nine. His other obligations have been thoroughly examined in preceding chapters of this book and therefore my focus should not be interpreted as an attempt to trivialize them. Further, the application of Deming's obligations to higher education in general, and to continuing private higher education in particular is developmental as we look for opportunities to permeate the academic, service and management sub-cultures of our institutions with continuous improvement policies and strategies. What should be most clear to all of us in these discussions is the goal of total quality learning.

CHARACTERISTICS OF PRIVATE HIGHER EDUCATION

The distinguishing characteristics of private post-secondary institutions in contrast to their public counterparts are less sharp than 50 or 100 years ago. First, private colleges and universities are still tuition driven but today require substantial endowments and sophisticated fund raising strategies to survive. Typically, they have had to be rather well tuned to their graduates, maintaining warm, friendly, personal relationships with them. At the same time, these contacts paid off with generous contributions. These same institutions experienced escalating institutional costs and as a result were driven to business and industry seeking additional support. For private institutions, fund raising is a tradition. On this point there is little distinction between publics and privates. Both face costs that outstrip tuition and both are competing for additional support from major corporations.

Second, most private institutions were church affiliated in their early history and though many have abandoned it, this religious identity permits, if not obligates them, by definition, to instill and advocate personal and community spirituality. It further requires them to take positions on ethical, moral, and social issues.

Third, private schools tend to be smaller, more personal and less bureaucratic. Students feel important, listened to and cared for. Less bureaucracy gives smaller private schools an edge in responding to the marketplace, which in recent decades has demanded "practitioner" degrees, or non-research, application oriented degrees offered in the evening and on weekends.

Fourth, private institutions are generally free of public monetary control. Tuition, spending levels and salaries are all determined internally.

Fifth, private institutions have in the past tended to reward effective teaching and faculty rather than research and publications. But a new trend is emerging. Small to medium sized private colleges and universities, feeling the pressure to attract scholarly faculty and to force "retired" faculty still on the payroll to produce and stay current are adopting new policies which require writing and research.

Sixth, most private higher education institutions were typically liberal arts focused. They required more than half of all undergraduate courses for graduation to be non-major courses and included philosophy and theology. Some still do.

In the main, these characteristics continue to distinguish most private institutions. Admittedly, there are exceptions and even some glaring exceptions, such as fund raising. But over time there has been a drift toward the secularization of private schools. These discussions, I believe, are coming at the right and perfect time. Private continuing higher education can be a catalyst for creating a better integration of learning and teaching while at the same time searching for more effective ways of integrating the content and spirit of liberal arts throughout the fabric of society.

DEMING'S OBLIGATIONS

Enter Deming. It is well within the realm of possibility that Deming's obligations, applied to private institutions, could be the revolutionary vision to rekindle the passion for differentiation on which they were founded but from which some have drifted toward a less distinguishable center. It is with this spirit that I read his fourteen obligations and I invite colleagues of private institutions to re-examine quality through Deming's system as a means to further distinguish their remarkable histories and futures; to continuously improve and integrate learning and teaching; and continually improve our society, making it a safe, healthy and supportive place for all of us.

1.   Create constancy of purpose towards improvement of product and service, with the aim to be competitive, stay in business, and provide jobs.

There are two primary foci of this obligation applied to continuing higher education. First, the student is the most important focus in adult education; second, a continuous feedback loop assures that adult student needs are continually being addressed and improved.

Student Focus. Programs and services are designed to attract and retain working adults. They are created to meet adult needs, marketed to and for adults, tested by adults, scheduled for adults, evaluated by adults and where possible redesigned for adults. It sounds easy. It is not. The two most difficult challenges in private continuing education are to operationally define the needs of adult students for the rest of the institution which tends to be driven by and organized around the needs of traditional students; and pricing.

Therefore, to create institutions with a primary focus on students and in continuing education, on adult students, it is imperative that internal communication exist between and among the vice president for academic affairs, the academic dean, the dean of New College, the vice president for finance, the provost, the faculty, traditional and adult student organizations, and all support services. Without these levels of interaction firmly operative adult programs cannot remain competitive or offered at prices students and corporations are willing to pay. The imperative? In addition to knowing our students are and what they want we must also know our inquiries and applicants are and what they want. How do we get to know them and what they want? For Deming the answer is surveys -- the critical ingredient. Surveys, however, are a bit thorny. In addition to asking "What does the student want?" we must also ask, "What do they need?" The academic community possesses knowledge which adults need; students do not always know what knowledge they need to know. Do not misunderstand me. I do not suggest that college faculty have a corner on knowledge. Student and faculty alike bring knowledge to the classroom. But designing a program which elicits input from both questions is critical to the success of adult programs. A program centered around the ignorance of the adult student diminishes both the student and the institution. A program designed around the knowledge base and curiosity of an inquiring adult student and the explorative mind of an experienced instructor produces outcomes which exceed the expectations of both.

To be successful, in Deming's words, colleges need constancy of purpose which means better educated students. To achieve this goal, the president of the college and his administrative team must determine constancy of purpose. This is no less true in private liberal arts universities. The president must be committed to liberal arts/career-oriented undergraduate degree programs made available at times convenient to adults. To what end? To ensure that its graduates are imprinted with the values found in the liberal arts courses, including theology, philosophy, English, mathematics, science, social science and foreign languages; and to apply these values and technical knowledge to their environment. Therefore, managers in continuing private higher education should have as the primary outcome when establishing constancy of purpose, better educated students, curious students who are rewarded for asking the right questions and provided a forum in which they can be answered.

Paulo Freire, the noted Brazilian educator and human rights activist, accuses the United States education system of being authoritarian. At a conference in January 1990 (Augsburg College, Minneapolis), he went a step further and called it a form of tyranny. Our system, he said, provides answers to students who have not asked questions; and questions that they do ask go unanswered. Many students learn only the answer to exam questions (Freire, pg. 34-43). Blanket indictments of education such as Freire's cause discomfort to some of us but they can serve as catalysts to use Deming's obligations to initiate needed reform. He goes on. Bureaucratization of education, he says, means adaptation with minimal risk, with no surprises and no questions. Result? A pedagogy of answers which is a pedagogy of adaptation, not a pedagogy of creativity. It does not encourage people to take the risk of inventing, or re-inventing. (Freire, pg. 40).

Freire says, in fact, that our educational system is like a production line where the process is more efficient when workers ask few questions, and perform only the task required at their station. No questions. No curiosity. No mistakes. No change. No growth. No risks. No surprises. No discovery. That is not the way we like to view programs or services in private colleges. Like it or not, his indictment is a challenge. Whether he is right or wrong is less important than his challenge to continually improve what we do, or what we think we do. The bottom line is to ask the right questions and make sure the ambient is present for faculty and students to continually question and explore possible answers if the system is to work.

Constancy of purpose, if it means better educated students, should evoke questions on our part as administrators related to what we offer and how to improve it. Is the program better this year than it was last year in meeting student needs? Is it more effective or efficient today than yesterday?

Continuous Feedback Loop. Deming's continuous feedback loop is a vital part of his emphasis on quality. He replaces the old model of design it, make it, try to sell it with this continuous feedback loop. It calls for designing a product, making and testing it on a production line, putting it on the market, testing it in service, and then finding out why people use it or not. Using continuous feedback from students and employers who hire our graduates builds in a mechanism for examining both the quality of our credit and non-credit programs, as well as academic support services.

2. Adopt a new philosophy. We are in a new economic age, created by Japan. Western management must awaken to the challenge, must learn their responsibility, and take on leadership for change.

Deming was unable to sell his fourteen obligations to the American auto industry with its post-war monopoly on automobile manufacturing even though monopolies, as William Ouchi points out in his book, The M Form Society, set the stage for superstitious learning.

"Under monopoly, management can be remiss and the workers can be inefficient, yet the company will have greater sales and earnings each year. Everyone concerned will `learn' that they know how to run the business and make money. That learning, however, is entirely superstitious and bares no relation to reality" (Scherkenbach, pp. 16-17).

Further, he says,

"It takes a big jolt for people to understand that the old philosophy will not be adequate in the new economic age, and still a bigger jolt to persuade them to accept the new philosophy . . . It takes a calamity to get their attention. Dr. Samuel Johnson said that nothing heightens a man's senses like the prospect of being hanged in the morning. Japan lost a military war; its peoples backs were against the wall; their only resources were people and willing management . . ." (Scherkenbach, pg. 17).

Unfortunately higher education is oftentimes slow to adopt any new philosophy and we are comfortable with this reluctance as the designated repositories of knowledge and preservers of history and tradition. In the end, time will require education to be more inclusive of discovery and creativity.

When institutions accept preservation as a dominant focus they pay a high price. For example, a private post-secondary Minnesota institution, while desperately preserving its past, closed because it failed to recognize the new economic age. If different questions had been asked over the last twenty-five years, questions which recognized the new economic age, it would still be in the education mainstream. It gives all of us a reason to wonder about the unasked questions. Did they lack the courage to ask difficult questions? Did they lack the courage to change?

What does all of this mean to private continuing higher education? I recognize that the auto industry is not a proper or adequate metaphor for education, but the message is clear. Education requires leadership to ask the right questions which clearly define its purpose with faculty, administrators and staff so that all share a common understanding of its constancy of purpose and will to achieve its purpose. Obviously, clearer focus makes for happier faculty, happier administration, happier support staff and happier students.

However, whether in a secular or sacred tradition, the lure is usually toward preservation. As we learn to maneuver safely within our tradition we feel safe and protected. But those of us in church-related institutions must not only know our traditions, we must search for the spirit of those traditions for new applications today.

Scherkenbach observes that, ". . . Dr. Deming's philosophy is not widely accepted in America (because) it calls for a major change, revolution, if you will. It is a pity that people usually take the path of least resistance" (Scherkenbach, pg. 22). Later, he quotes Don Peterson, Chairman of the Ford Motor Company, as he opened a Deming seminar in 1982 for senior management at Ford . . . "As I was thinking about this meeting, it struck me strongly that you are the ones who are going to decide if we are really successful in making a dramatic change in how we do business. You are the ones . . . It can be very difficult to make significant changes, especially when you have been in the habit of doing things differently, and especially when the very success that brought you to the positions you now hold was rooted in doing some things, frankly, the wrong way. It is going to be hard for you to accept that-- that you were promoted for the wrong reasons a time or two."

Being wrong at the level Peterson describes above can be made right only from the top down. It requires a systemic change, a new philosophy.

Scherkenbach comments that, "the (auto) industry had become accustomed to running their businesses by watching each other . . . If you try to meet the competition, you will not survive in this new economic age. You must try to meet the customer, not just the competition . . . It is you who must change, not the competition" (Scherkenbach, pg. 23). The challenge is to reinterpret the mandate of our institutions by capturing the essence of our history and purpose as well as the knowledge and skill needed by students today but challenged by a tomorrow which promises to be quite different.

We in adult education cannot assume that we know what students need or want without asking. Nor can we impose knowledge on them as Freire says, and create a new kind of tyranny, a tyranny of imposing answers on students who have not asked the questions. The questions we ask are critical. Are we preservationists and, therefore, venturi tubes which simply pass on information and knowledge or are we integrationists who integrate the past with the present and future?

3 . Improve constantly and forever the system of production and service, to improve quality and productivity and thus constantly decrease costs.

Building quality into our programs means among other things: selecting experienced and accomplished faculty who combine mastery of a discipline and mastery of the art of teaching; admitting students who are ready for the academic and personal journey provided through an adult undergraduate education; and using mid-term course evaluations and focus groups.

Faculty. The faculty selection process is at best difficult because it requires identifying technically competent professionals who simultaneously possess effective interactive teaching skills, knowledge of and experience with working adult students, knowledge of and use of a variety of learning styles, ability to view himself/herself as a living resource to students and not primarily as a lecturer, and the skills to stimulate curiosity, inventiveness, and exploration. Adult students seldom shrink back from demanding faculty who engage them. They welcome those who are passionate about their subject area, expect them to be and complain when they are not. Our responsibility is to find women and men with solid academic histories and credentials who can ignite, evoke and demonstrate by their teaching and scholarship the attributes of a lifelong learner.

If these attributes are lacking in either full-time or adjunct faculty, adult program administrators should be organizing workshops for faculty to learn more effective teaching strategies.

Students. Adults are either beginning or returning to college. Those just beginning frequently lack confidence that they can be successful as a college student. Those returning not infrequently carry with them unsuccessful academic histories. In either situation, experienced academic advisors must respond to both the student and the person. The advisors in this program, through a series of skillful questions, try to determine the students personal and professional goals, refer them to career or personal counselors when appropriate, attempt to determine whether their level of determination is appropriate to the demands of the program, attempt to determine if the program will accurately address the student's stated or implied needs. In all cases we recommend that they explore other programs as well so that when they do apply to New College they will be relatively certain that this is the best program to help them reach their goals.

By being meticulous about this level of quality control, we assure that a higher percentage of students will get what they want and need. A satisfied student is a far better program representative than one who is mismatched and complains endlessly to all who will listen. Some may argue that institutions cannot afford to turn away mismatched students. They need the revenue. If Deming is to be taken seriously, however, we have to provide what students need. This means we have to improve our current program or invent new programs to enhance student productivity.

Mid-term Course Evaluations. Most institutions of higher learning use end-of-term student evaluations as a means of addressing quality control. So do we. But we also use mid-term evaluations. Students use them as an opportunity to reinforce those things the instructor is teaching or doing which positively contribute to the learning process and to comment on those things which seemingly frustrate the learning process. These comments are available at a time when improving changes can be made which will enrich the experience of students and instructor.

Similarly, the type of evaluation form used is critical to the process. Evaluation forms which provide only a numeric value at the end of the semester are useless as evaluation instruments though they may be helpful in determining salary increments.

Many faculty argue that students are incapable of evaluating them as faculty. It is true that students normally are ill-prepared to evaluate an instructor's subject mastery. However, they normally are well prepared to evaluate teaching effectiveness and clarity of presentation. Given that, are the adult students always right if they are critical of an instructor? Of course not! Should an instructor always do or not do what students suggest on evaluation forms? Of course not! There must be room for professional judgment. But where to draw the line? Where does professional judgment stop or start?

The real questions in continuing higher education must always be: Are students learning? Are they learning content? Are they learning integration? Are they learning application? Are they discussing and learning from one another? Are they learning to share, grow and change within group discussion? Are they challenging themselves and the instructors to go beyond where they are? Are their knowledge and experiences considered important ingredients in the classroom?

To the extent that these questions are continually addressed by both faculty and adult students, the learning process is alive. Evaluation instruments in turn must address these same questions if the learning is to be enhanced.

Focus Groups. Focus groups composed of current adult students and recent graduates provide more thorough strategies for assessing the quality of student experiences with respect to the academic program, student services, advertising and promotional materials, and availability of staff for advising and referral. This is an opportunity for the dean to listen -- not to comment or defend -- just listen. Outcomes from these groups can easily be incorporated into goals and objectives for the following year. Students welcome the opportunity to be part of this evaluation process, are surprised by the invitation, contribute reflectively and passionately, and are always grateful to be included.

There are numerous quality control strategies available to constantly improve the content and process of undergraduate adult programs. Whatever strategy is used the goal is to improve both because both require improvement. Even programs and services doing well can be improved -- and should be. The old bromide, "Don't fix it if it ain't broke" is counter-productive to continuous improvement and should be eliminated from our vocabulary.

4. Remove barriers that rob the hourly worker of his right to pride of workmanship. The responsibility of supervisors must be changed from sheer numbers to quality. Remove barriers that rob people in management and engineering of their right to pride of workmanship. This means, inter alia, abolishment of the annual merit rating and of management by objectives.

Scherkenbach provides considerable detail about three practices in the workplace which inhibit pride of workmanship: performance appraisal systems; daily production reports; and the financial management system. Each in its own way destroys team work, encourages mediocrity, focuses on the short-term, and not infrequently promotes dishonesty. Of performance appraisals he says, they "are ineffective, inaccurate, unnecessary and often embarrassing . . ." (Scherkenbach, pg. 52). These systems frequently place units and individuals in competition with each other and, therefore, contribute to low self-esteem, low morale, and little ownership and/or pride in the product or process. Whereas, "The principal purpose of an appraisal and development system should be to nurture and sustain individual employee contributions to continuous improvement . . . (It) should be based on a deep regard for people and recognize that employees are the organization's most important resource. The system should contribute to the development and motivation of all employees . . . (It) will require a continuous effort in counseling, coaching and honest, open communications between the employee and supervisor, supported by opportunities for enhancement of professional, managerial and interpersonal skills" (Scherkenbach, pg. 57).

It sounds good, maybe ideal. Most of us in adult continuing education could not find a single idea with which to disagree. But my sense is that for many, even in church related institutions, this Deming obligation is a distant reality. Where to begin? First, begin where you have control of the system. For example, recognize/remove inhibitors to pride of workmanship in your own office and with faculty and students in your program. Recognize formally and informally when jobs are well done. Phone calls and letters of appreciation, recognition lunches all draw attention to students and faculty who take continuous improvement seriously and who take pride in their accomplishments. If faculty are involved on committees, as the Edinborough/Mississippi State University document suggests, take their reports seriously and implement their recommendations. If their recommendations are of such a nature that they cannot be supported financially or philosophically then further discussions are necessary to arrive at compromise solutions (pg 124).

Second, this same document suggests that professional work plan agreements for each faculty member be adopted to include all teaching, research and service assignments and projects focused on improvement in the quality of education. Though this exercise could feel repressive to faculty initially, with appropriate communication between the faculty and the administration they will contribute to a clearer university-wide understanding of constancy of purpose and to the implementation of a continuous improvement loop for adult programs all of which will result in higher levels of professional pride of accomplishment.

In general, continuing education administrators should provide opportunities for every employee to learn about the application of Deming's principles to education. Without system-wide immersion in this new process programs will seldom be evaluated with constancy of purpose clearly in focus. Eventually, the program will become self-serving to faculty and administrators needs but will have increasingly less relevance for adult students.

In all transactions whether they be faculty with students, or administration with faculty, or administration with students - pride of workmanship is a central spoke attached to the hub of improving the quality of student learning. Everything in adult continuing education, whether it be the admission process, student recognition and awards, faculty recognition and feedback, the bottom line should be pride of workmanship. Knowing what is required to complete a project, having the proper resources and/or equipment, and designing an evaluation and reward system are basic building blocks in adult programs. For example, each one of us can evaluate our own annual performance review systems and ask how this process is contributing to the pride of each person reporting to us. We need to listen when employees or students describe the obstacles they encounter in the system. Often our first response is to defend the system. But learn to listen. Listen carefully to the problem. Ascertain if the system is blocking student or employee growth. Invite recommendations. Listen to and study their recommendations. Act on them as quickly as possible. Fear grows in institutions and programs without ears. Today, with new alternative adult programs springing up overnight to meet growing and changing demands, we must be resolute to keep focused on pride of workmanship and not get stuck in our own traditions.

5. Drive out fear so that everyone may work effectively for the company.

"No one can put in his best performance unless he feels secure" (Deming, ESU/MSU, pg. 85). "Security," says Deming, "means without fear or care -- not afraid to express ideas, not afraid to ask questions" (Deming, Walton, pg. 72). As in creating constancy of purpose, chief administrators in continuing higher education have an equally critical role in driving out fear in their institutions. The ESU/MSU document is singularly helpful in suggesting specific actions and attitudes which, if adopted, can significantly reduce fear. I have taken the liberty of creating two lists from this document of what administrators should and should not do.

To drive out fear from their institutions administrators should:

o   be predictable and make their positions known

o   compromise and avoid either precedent or tradition;

o   possess integrity by being frank and honest;

o   know that integrity assures that as things seem to be, so they are;

o   trust themselves without letting their ego or image get in the way;

o   bring out the best in others through recognition and encouragement;

o   be active listeners, giving others the gifts of respect, attention and recognition;

o   talk about projects they are working on;

o   maintain a sense of humor;

o   be change agents who work with groups;

o   recognize stress and minimize causes;

o   be adept in conflict management, not conflict resolution;

o   serve as facilitators rather than judge or arbitrator in conflict management;

o   be skilled in assumption analysis;

o   eliminate merit pay;

o   relate a compelling image of a desired state of affairs to the university community;

o   understand that communication creates meaning for people in higher education;

o   understand that success in higher education institutions depends on the existence of shared meanings and interpretations of reality;

o   know that shared meanings in higher education means that knowing why is more important in knowing how;

o   look at relative viewpoints rather than absolutes;

    o   understand that skin color, nationality, birth place, political belief, sex, financial status, and intelligence are not measures of worth or worthiness;

    o   praise in public, chastise in private.

To drive out fear from their institutions administrators should NOT:

    o   ridicule or use sarcasm;

    o   belittle, demean, or humiliate;

    o   express hostility or prejudice;

    o   try to eliminate conflict but consider it as a necessity in a highly differentiated institution;

    o   assess blame;

    o   differentiate between staff members and board members in showing respect and honesty.

Adult Programs. These guidelines apply equally to administrators in adult programs. Since the average age of adult students in many of our programs is 30, respect, equality, integrity, honesty, warmth and openness take on new meaning. When they are absent or in short supply, adult students will demand being treated as adults, not children or adolescents. Most policies and procedures at colleges and universities were created to manage adolescents. Conflict! We in adult programs understand the cause of the conflict and press for changes to accommodate adults. But many others believe the adult programs should conform to policies and procedures created for the traditional program.

In managing these intra-institutional conflicts we are both participants in and managers of the conflict. Not always an easy or appreciated position. None-the-less, it is reality for most of us. It is also essential to accept incremental progress toward goals which permit both traditionalists and innovators to win. It also creates incubation time for the innovations to be accepted and owned by many others. Some of us in church related institutions grew up believing that conflict is destructive and should be avoided at all costs, which means we are bereft of the necessary tools to conduct business. Higher education, particularly the academic deans and vice presidents, are at the very vortex of conflict. The preservationist/traditionalist and the innovators meet there to transact business for scarce resources and to decide mission focus. Conflicts are inevitable. What is required is better understanding of conflict. If one judges oneself lacking necessary tools to transact business, it is imperative to enroll in conflict management workshops ASAP. Without a profound and working understanding of conflict management, progress will inevitably be one sided and programs stalled.

We fear what we do not know. What we do not know we do not trust. The goal is to create systems of mutual trust, not necessarily of mutual agreement, but of trust. Unfortunately, the religious tradition of some private institutions exacerbate this fear of change. One of our tasks is to find ways for learning as a journey and faith as a journey to intersect.

Walton notes that, "People are afraid to point out problems for fear they will start an argument, or worse, be blamed for the problem. Moreover, so seldom is anything done to correct problems that there is no mechanism for problem-solving. Suggesting new ideas is too risky. People are afraid of losing their raises or promotions, or worse, their jobs. They fear punitive assignments or other forms of discrimination and harassment. They are afraid that superiors will feel threatened and retaliate in some fashion if they are too assertive or ask too many questions. They fear for the future of their company and the security of their jobs. They are afraid to admit they made a mistake, so the mistake is never rectified. In the perception of most employees, preserving the status quo is the only safe course." (Walton, pg. 72).

In our transactions with staff, other university personnel and in every communication with our adult students we should be asking how is what I am doing, saying or writing creating a stronger bond of trust with that person. If it is not, then we should stop doing it, reassess, redesign and begin again. Trust is the only foundation upon which healthy adult programs can be built.

WHERE DO WE GO FROM HERE?

Deming is not the third tablet off of Sinai. But his management method is a vehicle to reassess what, why and how we do what we do in private continuing higher education. His methods provoke questions and his questions provoke change. If we want to impact society at formative levels as our mission statements indicate, then Deming is a good match. But if not Deming, find other ways to elevate continuous improvement as the core focus of your continuing education program and your institutions.

REFERENCES

Cornesky, Robert A., et.al. Deming: New Directions for Improving Quality, Public Acceptance and Competitive Positioning in Colleges and Universities, Edinboro University, Edinboro, PA, January 1989.

Freire, Paulo and Faundez, Antonio. Learning to Question, A Pedagogy of Liberation, 1989.

Ireland, John. "The Mission of Catholics in America." Speech at the 100th Anniversary of John Carroll, November 1889, Published in The Church and Modern Society, Vol. I of II, 1896.

Scherkenbach, William W. The Deming Route to Quality and Productivity, Road Maps and Roadblocks, 1988.

University of St. Thomas Catalog, 1990-1992.

CHAPTER FIVE

COMMUNITY COLLEGES AND QUALITY ENHANCEMENT
Rick P. Williamson

The economic development roles of community colleges and businesses are entwined by the need for ever-improving quality.

Democracy is the most sought after privilege of modern times and is synonymous with growth and economic development worldwide. The foundation of a democracy is built on education. Education enables people to grapple with the complexities of a global economy and thus keep democracy strong (Lindeman, 1961).

Now when education is critical, there are signs in the U.S. that parts of the educational infrastructure are deteriorating and the world leadership role that our democracy has played may be threatened. It is time to assess what can be done to keep education strong through immediate repairs and ongoing improvements (Heslep, 1989).

At a time when democratic leadership is at a critical high, our elementary and secondary educational systems fall far short of what U.S. students need and a global society demands.

To provide an educational alternative or perhaps a stopgap measure, community colleges emerged to deal with some of the inadequacies fostered by our out-dated elementary and secondary education system.

INTRODUCTION

Democracy. Democracy has become the most sought after privilege of modern times and is synonymous with growth and economic development worldwide. It is an accepted fact that the foundation of a democracy is built on education. Without education and the ability of the population to grapple with the complexities of a global economy, the strength of a democracy is threatened (Lindeman, 1961).

At a time when education is so needed, there are signs in the U.S. that parts of the educational infrastructure are deteriorating and the world leadership role that our democracy has played may be threatened. It is time that we all look at education and assess what can be done to keep it strong through immediate repairs and ongoing improvements (Heslep, 1989).

Past is not Prologue. When the various levels of U.S. education are analyzed, higher education has consistently been the strongest part of the total educational system. This educational leadership has been essential in the role that the U.S. has played in all facets of global development. Foreign nations continue to send their best and brightest students to American shores for an education which has been second to none. Today, higher education is being stretched and tested daily by a global marketplace, the explosion of knowledge and innovations, the exponential expansion of technology, and the preparedness of college age U.S. students.

Outdated System. Starting at about age five, children move through a prescribed regimen of programs influenced by a variety of social, political, and educational forces which seek to mold each child into a contributing member of society. It is clear, however, that there are weaknesses in these early educational stages. Former strategies for bringing a student through the twelve years (actually less than six years when total "real" instructional time is calculated) of elementary and secondary school no longer work or are inadequate for many students. Many schools in the orient and to some extent in Europe, demand and get much more from their students. For example, a typical oriental high school student will go to school six days a week from 8:00 am to 6:00 pm with study assignments every evening. In a cross-national assessment of student achievement in high school mathematics, U.S. high school students scored lower in calculus than the students of any other industrial nation except British Columbia where high school calculus is not taught. This fact is still true if you compare only the top one percent of the high school students (Harris, 1989).

The weakness of the U.S. system is cause for concern to every person in our democracy. A North Carolina firm run by Mitsubishi found that in order to meet their goal to have all their workers possess a basic knowledge of statistical techniques, they had to hire American students with graduate degrees. In Japan, any high school graduate would have the same knowledge.

At a time when democratic leadership is at a critical high, our elementary and secondary educational systems fall far short of what U.S. students need and a global society demands.

Illiteracy, dropping out, low motivation, school paralysis, parental dysfunction, economics, and many other "factors" contribute to the creation of college age students who are not as prepared or as competitive in the work environment as their foreign counterparts. Instead, they appear to be resting on "use-to-be" and "you-owe-me". The scenario witnessed by a new material start-up plant is unfortunately repeated throughout the country on a scale that is unbelievable. Motorola wanted to hire about 200 people with tenth-grade level skills but could only find about 60 who could meet minimal performance standards (Harris, 1989). Other companies have set criteria to hire only high school or GED graduates to find that the available labor pool will not support their need.

No wherein our educational system is quality taught, yet we expect quality in everything we buy. Numerous studies have shown that Americans will buy quality even though we have learned that personal attention to quality is not a priority. In a way, it is a lack of maturity. As we foster the growth of our children, we try to teach them a variety of skills by letting them experiment and learn by doing. Children going through this process learn that making mistakes is okay and quality is of little or no concern since it is expected that the parent will follow behind the child to inspect and correct. There is nothing wrong with this process since trying and failing are important parts of working and succeeding. Unfortunately, this process follows children through elementary and secondary school and into the work place. In the work place there is no parent or teacher to follow- up, to ensure that a quality service or product has been provided. Each worker must be able to ensure his or her own quality.

The out-dated "follow-up thinking" in our homes, and perpetuated by elementary and secondary education, produces an unqualified worker and thereby increases the probability that the mantel of progress and growth will be passed on to others (foreign countries) who are willing to take on the quality challenges of our exciting and expanding world.

It is not that Americans are incapable of learning and performing on the job. Time has proven just the opposite. For example, a Chicago based television plant was recording a defect rate of 31 percent until a Japanese firm bought the firm -- retrained and managed the existing workers, supervisors, and middle management -- and reduced the defect rate to 6 percent. Workers in Nissan's Tennessee plant meet or exceed the quality of work done by Nissan workers in Japan (Harris, 1989).

Educators, facing these problems, have looked at the growing number of non-productive students and have seen that many of them are unable to further their learning due to lack of preparation in elementary and secondary schools and/or the unwillingness of students to venture past their own front doors to obtain the educational background needed to make them vital parts of society.

To provide an educational alternative or perhaps a stopgap measure, a relatively new educational option has emerged to deal with some of the inadequacies fostered by our out-dated elementary and secondary education system.

This cost advantaged, community and human resource is the **community college.**

COUNTERPARTS

Pictured by many of its students as a convenient aid to taking the important step from secondary to higher education, the community college continues to struggle as the "mister-in-between," the four year college's "step child," and the "clean-up" department for elementary and secondary schools.

The community college has quickly become a recognizable force in the American educational picture. Enrolling approximately 50 percent of all higher education students, community colleges are providing the students with chances for remediation, academic and vocational alternatives, new starts in life, and avenues for preparing for their difficult global future (Brint & Karabel, 1989).

While community colleges seek new directions in higher education, business and industry leaders also struggle with change. Businesses which want to exist in the next century know that they must be closely linked to training and education. Technology, a changing world economy, and an underprepared workforce have forced business and industry to evaluate their workforce and provide education and training.

IT IS COST EFFECTIVE TO EDUCATE. These words ring true in every successful business, industry, agency, organization, and institution. In economic terms, it is supply and demand -- there is a great demand for knowledgeable leaders and workers to improve processes, and there is an unparalleled opportunity to supply knowledge for future leaders.

No longer can the goals of business, industry, and education be viewed as divergent perspectives. Knowledge, information, education, and training, must be able to freely cross from business to education and back with one goal in mind: **PROVIDING QUALITY EDUCATION THAT WILL PRODUCE A QUALITY WORK FORCE WHICH ROUTINELY PRODUCES AND PROVIDES QUALITY PRODUCTS AND SERVICES FOR A GLOBAL MARKETPLACE.** Quality is the essential common denominator of business/industry and education. Quality is a means of defining customer fitness for use. Whether the product is education or business oriented, it must be directed toward improved product quality, cost effectiveness, and globally integrated into organizational activities (Moore, 1977). If higher education is to maintain its global leadership position, new directions need to be investigated and researched so that change can take place.

Change. Community colleges are facing some of the same choices initially presented to business and industry in the 1950s and now being faced by progressive business and industry leaders. Management philosophies need to change. More attention to quality needs to be built into the system. Everyone on the campus needs to become obsessed with new directions for excellence. Community colleges need to find ways to continue to be the world's best supplier of the most needed commodity in the world today -- Education.

By understanding and questioning various concepts such as Deming's principles, community college leaders can stretch their minds, question, brainstorm, plan for a new future, consider the relevance of these concepts, compare various alternatives, apply compatible concepts to their college mission, and raise the overall level of community college thinking. Community colleges have the opportunity to stand on the shoulders of others and enhance the quality of education with the promise and realization that when quality services are provided to students, quality students will be the positive end product.

Product. As any other business, community colleges have found that they must deliver a quality product. However, the community college product (student) brings to the college a large number of variables. She/he has the ability, the flexibility, and the right, to change at any moment in response to any of the countless stimuli. Nonetheless, if community colleges are to produce a "value-added" student/product, the educational process and all the processes that affect the student/product outcome must be preoccupied with the quality of the services provided to the student regardless of student/product variables.

Setting quality goals and instituting changes in the processes that can produce improved quality can be difficult and cannot be based solely on the perceptions of either external or internal groups. Whatever these perceptions are, there must be a dedication to quality education, to improved instructional practices, to excellence in program administration, and, most importantly, to the quality of the students who pass through the classes. Deming's 14 points give the community college some helpful direction.

DEMING'S POINTS

Improve Service. The journey to institutional dedication to quality is endless. When each person within the community college examines his/her sphere of influence by looking at the quality of service and the quality of product, it is possible to improve overall services and products continually.

Many academic terms mask the reality of the service - product relationship in higher education. This relationship, however, must be understood at its basic level so that systematic analysis of what is being done and how it is being done can be performed. In many cases this means spiral or incremental improvement through innovation. Whatever form innovation takes it must be productive. This means figuring out exactly what your purpose is, determining to what extent you are failing to achieve that purpose, and then finding specific, practical steps which will enable the institution to come closer to its purpose/mission. Identifying these steps is only part of it, however. There must be a positive correlation between the institutional purpose and the curriculum. Without this alignment, common direction cannot be fulfilled. In successful business, the mission is tied to product/service and vice versa. If, for example, it is the mission of an institution to assist students, why do we "serve" them so poorly in many of our registration procedures? In a Kentucky community college, it was found that 31 percent of the students who left did so because they were frustrated with the registration process (Harris, 1989).

In continuing education, there are many ways for educators to assist in this alignment and in fulfillment of the college mission. The first step is to harness the energy of a program leader who has vision. Many who aspire to be leaders are unable to look past today's tasks to tomorrow's needs and opportunities. Few educators have this ability, but it is the life blood of any viable education program. When a visionary leader is present, things will happen today which will make things happen tomorrow; without visionary management, things will still happen, but seldom with a clear and exciting plan that ties needs and aspirations of the present to the future.

Even when visionary community college continuing education leaders are found they cannot be all things to all people. This syndrome is a quagmire in which continuing education leaders find themselves when the demand for diversity in services and products expands. A seemingly impossible task of meeting these demands may be alleviated through the development of partnerships, consortiums, and alliances with others on and off-campus. These types of arrangements happen all the time in successful business and industry. Cooperative efforts with other departments, agencies, organizations, and institutions can become valuable alternatives. Professionals will find themselves spawning new possibilities and establishing organizational relationships that will eventually uncover new ways to improve service to students and help produce a quality product.

Many higher education administrators fail to see the advantage for cooperative relationships due to their preoccupation with "turf" and generating FTEs. Such narrow thinking in community colleges and specifically in continuing education fosters loss of focus and energy in the program.

Cooperative work on many educational fronts to meet community needs, agency shortcomings, student remediation, business and industry demands, and college student interests, dictates the down playing of institutional and departmental competition. Cooperative program coordination should be established as the rule rather than the exception. Why duplicate resources of personnel, time, facilities, marketing, development, and instructors unnecessarily, when, through cooperative dialogue and planning, more needs can be met in a more expeditious, cost effective manner?

Often, the simple economics of program offerings are enough to drive continuing education programs toward program cooperation. Today, the high quality of programming demanded by students dictates that duplication of the "tools" needed to provide quality services, whether they be capital assets, facilities, personnel, or others, must be eliminated to alleviate programs that waste public and private dollars.

After leadership has been evaluated and cooperation established, the college professionals need to direct their attention to the improvement of classroom services -- the nucleus of the educational process. Higher education is dealing with quality in the classroom more than ever before, however, much remains to be done, especially in outreach programs. Students in these programs are making sacrifices to reach their educational goals. Planning and budgeting for appropriate student-teacher ratios, identifying facilities that promote learning, and locating classes and learning resources that are convenient to students all affect student/product quality.

New Philosophy. Much can be said for the leadership role that American higher education has taken throughout modern history, but the future is uncertain. A new global philosophy which prepares students for a global society must be realized.

The change should begin with updated organizational attitudes and institutional understanding of the impact on students of technology, economic development, foreign influence, world economy, and the fast pace of change.

Technological change is not a new phenomenon, nor is the exponential rate of growth that surrounds technological development. Institutions must also understand the impact of foreign progress and influence on the total educational equation. In the past, it was not necessary for higher education to keep a daily record of development off American shores. Progress was slow and predictable, non-threatening, and inconsequential.

Today, with the increased flow of information, continuing education programs must reflect a contemporary world picture if we are to satisfactorily serve our students and participate in the local imperative of economic development. Just as business ignored Deming in the 1950s, there are still many businesses where it is equally hard for educators to convince managers and workers that they are undereducated and under informed and ill-prepared for the future. It is difficult for continuing education to run programs for an audience that desperately needs assistance in preparing for the future when the audience perceives no need.

Perhaps the best method to facilitate and lead change is to ask educators and educational programs to put forth the best example possible. Programs must include internationalization of the curriculum, ranging from millimeters to foreign languages, from knowledge about foreign materials and goods to new management and monetary polices. The key is to create an environment which fosters a "spirit to improve" (Harris, 1989). Approaches need to include reeducation of educators, instructing professors, and training administrators. These approaches foster up-to-date curriculum developments, modification of college guidelines, and improved teaching techniques.

All of this means that the new philosophy must encompass how educational services are perceived and presented as well as how the business of higher education is managed. Managing the programs is much like walking a tight rope and balancing what needs to be done to prepare for the future with the fiscal crises and the operational realities of the day. Continued and expanded cooperation between education and business in terms of real dollar support is vital.

Inspection. Higher education's proclivity to assess, analyze, and evaluate continually is contrary to Deming who suggests that quality cannot be dependent on inspection and that inspection needs to be eliminated. The 1950s generation of business and industry probably found the elimination of inspection a hard a pill to swallow when they first reviewed Deming. Today, educators are looking at the same medicine (Glasser, 1990). One must ask whether it would be desirable if our educational system ran so that every person was pre-occupied with excellence and quality? Relying on others to improve quality does not make it possible for each person to develop his/her own systematic approach to establishing individual control of the product or service (Harris, 1989). Everyone needs to be dedicated to the absolute best quality educational services possible and producing the highest quality student/product possible. If this mind set were adopted, the almost exhaustive efforts which are now spent to prepare and present assessment documentation could be eliminated and those efforts redirected to the development and implementation of other quality systems.

In continuing education, the relationship between quality and the service/product are probably more closely tied together than in any other department. Hypothetically, if the need for a continuing education program is constant, it becomes simple economics -- supply and demand. Someone needs a service; education provides a quality service; if the service does not produce a quality student/product, the service is terminated. If the service can produce a student/product with increased worth, the service is judged "quality" and will perpetuate itself.

All of this suggests that community college continuing education programs stop looking at evaluation of services as an end. A system of quality control needs to be in place so that the performance of the services and products can be compared to the performance of established standards. When these standards are not met, corrective action needs to be pursued (Besterfield, 1979). If faculty and/or classroom instruction is maintained at a high level, then the most appropriate and most valuable evaluation is not of the overall process or the instructors that are part of the process but by the QUALITY MEASUREMENT of the end product i.e. the student! Ongoing, individualized, and personalized quality control by each faculty and administrative member is crucial to the continued improvement of the student/product. External inspection, however, is just that -- external -- and has questionable worth. Quality does not come from inspection but from improvement of the process through slow, continual, step-by-step realization of the institutional mission. Educators must start by accepting what is in place and then work individually to improve it incrementally until the end product is of the quality demanded (Harris, 1989).

When properly developed, self administered individualized quality control (evaluation) becomes tied to team (faculty) quality control which leads to increased quality and productivity resulting in product production without turn backs or defects. In industry, it is the job of each person on the team to produce quality products. Likewise, if the continuing educator accepts the professional obligation to ensure that thought and quality have been put into each detail of every program, then the quality student/product will be produced. The responsibility for quality can never be left up to, passed on to, or achieved by external sources; it must come from within each person.

Perhaps here the concept of "needs-based teaching" can be adopted. By teaching to needs, educational services, starting in the classroom, can be permitted to constantly change to meet student demands and the ever-changing external forces of our global society. If administrators of continuing education programs could constantly find ways of providing a needs based learning experience, then a "valued added" curriculum would be achieved.

Cost. In most instances, community college continuing education is the best buy in town -- for the student, for the business, and for the taxpayer. But price tag alone does not govern what consumers are willing to buy, nor should they or will they come to the community college solely on price tag merits. As providers of a service, community college continuing education must be willing to devote a large percentage of the program's attention to instilling quality in everything.

Symbiotic long term relationships among continuing education program service providers and local school systems, the community, businesses, and industries need to exist.

With school systems, great attention to cooperative articulation is essential so that college services can be brought to their classrooms and students can be assisted in finding a path to higher education.

Likewise, in the community, the community college continuing education must understand the culture, be able to focus on needs, and forecast changes so that quality programs can meet those needs. This task is never completely accomplished, but when efforts are made in the direction of greater community understanding, community college continuing education will come closer to being the single supplier or cooperative provider of educational services to the community.

There is great diversity in business and industry when it comes to training. The American Society of Training and Development estimates that major corporations spend more than $40 billion a year on training. In these major corporations, community colleges can play an important supportive role.

For the thousands of small to medium size businesses, the community college can be the sole supplier of quality training programs. The difficulty in becoming a single supplier of education to small and medium sized businesses lies in the usually unplanned and sometimes haphazard company training programs. Many business and industry programs need the assistance of professional educators with expertise in public relations, company needs assessment, and program development. After solid business relationships are established, identification of needs should take place, followed by an organized, easily implemented training plan orchestrated by community college continuing education professionals. When done correctly, this plan can bring new life and direction to a company, its employees, and their combined future which will include the improvement of the campus' bottom line.

Improving. Constantly improving is a theme that rings throughout Deming's philosophy and is a goal that all continuing educators can strive for in their work. Improvements can sometimes seem hard, however, it is imperative that management understand the need for daily, relentless pursuit of improvement (Amsden, 1988). Daily continuing education professionals must maintain a high energy and high interest level in their development and presentation of programs which many times can become mundane with repetitive overtones. With a myriad of program details, the work can become automatic without a sense of progress or accomplishment. Continuing educators need to see that improvement itself becomes an educational aim, that making things run more smoothly becomes a challenge, that more creativity and imagination can be built into every program, that the opportunity to lead and motivate can be fun, that a total program can become exciting if a sense of contagious enthusiasm is instituted, and that (perhaps most importantly) improvement occurs in ways that permits students to use education to meet their needs which will enable them to use their education as a change agent in their lives.

Daily improvements may be the best way to approach constant improvement in a community college continuing education program. If all professionals asked themselves each day what they could do new that would improve the quality of the programs, improvements would flourish and old thresholds cease to exist. However, some individuals find it hard to analyze a situation and determine avenues for improvement. For this segment of professionals, a quick look at the student/product input will probably bring reality to their doorstep.

The value of student input to improve quality cannot be refuted. Students are the products of the educational service and as close to the action as anyone is going to get. Students, especially adult "non-traditional" students, come with their own purpose and drive. They have little time for educational services that do not meet their needs or contribute positively to their lifelong learning mission. Few, if any, lack opinions of what is really happening, how good or bad something is, or on how educational services can be improved.

Faculty can help identify ways to improve. Too little communication takes place on many community college campuses among faculty, administration, division heads, and continuing educators. Yet faculty are vital to the quality, success, and improvement of continuing education programs; without them, nothing would happen. The focus, understanding, dedication, willingness, drive and excitement that faculty can bring to the classroom or distant learning environment is essential to quality.

Training. Skills only become habits through repetition and practice. New skills only develop when individuals take an active interest in what they are doing to the point that they seek new ways to improve and expand on their job abilities.

An organization dedicated to training on the job is usually an organization which takes a high interest in its human resources. The future of the organization rests on the shoulders of the professionals in the organization. Only a small part of our society has reached the point in their overall development to understand and accept that learning is a lifelong endeavor. Fortunately, higher education, on the whole, is in tune with this endeavor and realizes the importance of expanded learning in every facet of their lives: education, profession, family, spiritual, personal, societal -- everything.

The concept of lifelong learning needs to continue throughout adult life, including learning on the job. How can a community college grow if its most vital part -- the people -- do not progress and grow? Vigorous training programs must be instituted on the job. These programs need to address job skills, personal interests, current issues, family concerns, local and international matters, global awareness, and more. As part of on the job training, in-class programs need to be encouraged. All of these program areas and approaches, when made available to the college community, will help develop enhanced abilities on and off the job.

Off-campus, employee oriented companies need to make job site training opportunities available so that their employees and the company can learn and grow. These opportunities need to be made readily available. Many students in the community college cannot devote full time to academic or vocational pursuits. None the less, all students who need and want an education should be served by the educational system to the best of its ability. Job site training is an excellent place to start. When job site training is available, the logistical problems of location, time, convenience, and sometimes cost through company reimbursed programs are immediately solved for many. Viable continuing education programs will make this type of training available to companies and provide needed library, laboratory, financial, counseling, and other auxiliary services.

Offering training on the job before, during, and after work can help "job-bound" students become active in their own self improvement. When companies sponsor and support this type of training, a new positive team atmosphere can be created in the work place. Companies which have instituted in-house programs have had positive results in company productivity, worker attitude, corporate employee relations, and overall employee quality of life.

Leadership. Administrators must point the way toward continued improvement (Amsden, 1988). Leadership in a community college continuing education program can be perceived in many ways. It can be influence on others, charisma in personal contacts, dominance in program offerings, the magnetism that certain faculty have for students, the personalities of program administrators and faculty, the power to change people's lives, the strength of a program to deliver course work that meets student needs, the initiative of a program to deliver new and different alternatives, the influence of a program on the development of a region, or the initiative that individuals bring to a successful program.

Continuing Education programs which strive to incorporate these leadership qualities will find improvement in their total program excellence. Good leaders need to be supportive and stimulative of people's efforts, knowing when to lead out in front and knowing when to guide and assist those wishing to move ahead. They know when to stop and look around, to bring in the abilities, knowledge, and insight of others. When this environment is created in a continuing education program, all members of the staff will begin to devote time and effort to the identification of new audiences needing educational services. Additionally, they will see the need and benefit of spending time with program providers and end users to evaluate program quality.

Based on the Kaizen concept, each individual must motivate him/herself to have a genuine concern for: discipline, time management, skill development, participation and involvement, morale, and communications. A unified team approach using these elements will bring about improved program quality. Professional continuing educators involved in the process of identifying, instituting, and dealing with change will find it easier to work as a continuing education team (Imai, 1984).

The ability of a leader to manage change will many times dictate the ability of a continuing education program to react to community needs and be on the forefront of institutional program research and development -- pushing the barriers of tradition with innovation and creativity.

An American management leader recently stated that it was the manager's job to manage change and if the manager failed, management must be changed. Change is not always sudden or abrupt -- it needs to be gradual and deliberate. Whatever form that change takes, good leaders must first be able to plan for it, manage it on an ongoing basis, and react to unforeseen change when necessary. The higher the level of total leadership exhibited in a community college continuing education program, the greater the possibility for change management and program success.

Fear. Fear in the work place has almost become a way of life. In the past, employees could be assured of a job with a company or institution and expect to spend their life there. Today, with fiscal crises, demographic shifts, mergers, foreign competition, union strife, hostile takeovers and more, job security seems to be a thing of the past.

Academia, in program areas where productivity and results are measured, has its own type of fear built into the work place. Those within the system must produce FTEs, design money-making programs, fill faculty loads, be vital in the community, and be self supporting. All of this takes place in an atmosphere of unprecedented pressure from financial managers, politics, staff sizes, support faculty, college goals, and curriculum content.

A couple of fear- reducing alternatives for community college continuing education programs exist: (1) being realistic about local supply and demand for programs, whether they be on or off campus, credit or non-credit, for traditional or non-traditional students; and (2) resigning oneself (and everyone else) to work hard and be dedicated to providing the best quality educational services possible. Both alternatives sound simple but can be difficult.

First, unrealistic demands put on continuing education programs can lead to unsuccessful results. The philosophy that higher program volume plus smaller continuing education staffs will equal higher FTE and produce higher productivity just will not work. None of this will correlate with the quality paradigm. The need for continuing education programs grows daily, and it is impossible for community college continuing education staffs, even under the most perfect conditions, to meet the demand that is being placed on them. Therefore, educators must analyze the many needs in a community and strike a balance which will serve the largest array of the population with the best programs possible. Make the supply meet the most viable and pressing demands. Additionally, we need to involve students and empower them to be responsible for their own quality education.

Second, when each person within the community college continuing education program decides to work with a sense of dedication and seeks to provide the best educational services possible, requirements such as full-time equivalents, program quality, and program quantity will be natural outcomes. Unfortunately, such dedication cannot take place in the aforementioned environment of small staffs with expectations of high productivity. There must be space to allow for creativity and to avoid high levels of stress if the program is to advance.

Barriers. The power that lies in achieving synchronized and finely orchestrated continuing education programs can be exciting. However, individual units vary a great deal in their ability to achieve total program coordination and rarely does this happen at the institutional level.

Community college continuing education should be on the forefront of instituting institutional team work. The continuing education professional, who should be on the leading edge of institutional programming, needs academic and administrative support to foster solid program successes. When barriers are removed and professionals find ways of working together, synergistic power can move the institution to new possibilities.

Even when the institutional support is present, the great diversity of programs and individuals that the community college continuing education professional must deal with, demands great patients and wisdom. Communication is the key along with a generous understanding. The extreme differences that exist in an institution can either be its biggest asset or its biggest barrier.

It is the mission of continuing educators to involve as many campus professionals as possible in the initiation of ideas, the development of programs, and the implementation of concepts, so that everyone can see and feel that they are part of the end result. If the institutional barriers can be transcended, results will be more wide spread and recognition can go to many more individuals who can share in the fruits of the labor. If barriers emerge along the way or at the end, all those concerned need to work together to solve the problems or analyze their presence so that future endeavors can come closer to success.

Another alternative which can instill the "pride of workmanship" may include initiation of program incentives. Perhaps rewards can be given to faculty and others who are responsible for student recruitment. Based on the level of involvement and local guidelines, a fund could be made available to the most proactive contributors for professional development. Participation in program development and presentation might contribute to a professional's eligibility for free attendance to campus programs.

When barriers exist, they rob individuals of the rewards of completion, but when conventional thinking can be replaced by creative "imagineering", community colleges and continuing education programs will reap the rewards.

Exhortations. Deming suggest the elimination of exhortations and slogans pointing out that the use of exhortations and the setting of quotas can create an atmosphere of competition and adversarial relationships. A more positive approach suggests the development of a team environment where group support and institutional camaraderie are nurtured.

Everyone on campus needs to become involved in feeling and projecting a united positive image. This campus-wide representation and involvement should spread throughout the community including: business involvement, elementary and secondary school education, economic development, and in every course, workshop, seminar, or college activity.

As the community college continuing education program becomes a part of the community, institutional aloofness will be reduced, utilization of the college resources will become more integrated into community life, and the need for exhortations and quotes decreased.

Self-Improvement. Kaizen is the Japanese word for unending improvement. Community college continuing education programs would do well to institute the Kaizen concept to encourage self improvement. By creating an environment where teamwork, departmental synergism, and self-esteem are high priorities, an organization can achieve a high level of success both internally and externally (Heslep, 1989).

Thousands of books and tapes address the importance of improving the work-place and the importance of personal motivation and achievement. Community college continuing education programs should work with college administrators to stimulate and motivate those people on the campus who can make positive contributions to the continuing education effort by providing ways that those individuals can be involved in self-improvement activities.

A suggestion and support system that capitalizes on personal involvement, insight, and innovation should be instituted. Problem solving skills and enhanced job performance skills through cross education need to be considered. Resources of time and money should be made available to support self improvement.

There is a direct relationship between the amount of time and effort that is put into something and the benefit derived. If community college continuing education programs expect to offer programs that will lead the community and provide the educational foresight needed in today's changing world, then the programs must provide motivated professionals with the means to improve themselves in a way that will provide expanded opportunities to those being served.

It is not desirable to issue blank checks for any or all professional development or self- improvement activities. The institution and the continuing education program should only reward those professionals who support the stated institutional mission and the programs that will make it successful. Few apathetic individuals will be interested in continuing education centered self-improvement. Those professionals who wish to seek self-improvement which is divergent from the continuing education mission and vision should do so on their own.

Work. Work and the quality put into it are the key to any successful program. Work starts with dedication and understanding of one's role and the belief that one has the capability to positively affect student lives. This is an awesome responsibility which many cannot handle. Work should be defined by goals and through planned activities that outline a person's position and expectations, both personal and professional. Work in continuing education is at best a moving target. Yesterday's priorities are superseded by today's demands; tomorrow's plans are overshadowed by yesterday's mandates.

The rather hectic environment of continuing education has no room for individuals who feel "it is not my job" or "I do not get paid enough to do that." A total team effort must consume a community college continuing education program and become the nucleus from which a small idea has the possibility of becoming a multi-campus, multi-media, multi-program service opportunity.

This transformation is exciting, challenging, rewarding, but professionals who care only about putting in their time will find it very difficult. Individuals not interested in transforming work into services that will benefit the community, need to move aside and let the creative professionals breath new life into community college continuing education programs at a time when the world needs and demands quality education.

CONCLUSION

Higher education is at a point in its development that the world demands leadership and quality. The leaders in education now have the opportunity to choose what changes need to be made and the direction higher education will take. Only those institutions willing to lead the way in search of higher quality will be able to meet the increased needs of their students and of the world.

86

REFERENCES

Amsden, Robert T. and Davida M. Quality Circles, JIT, Deming Users, Juran Teams: The Link, Association for Quality and Participation, Cincinnati, Ohio 1987.

Berg, John, Team Building Techniques That Get Results, Association for Quality and Participation, Cincinnati, Ohio, 1987.

Besterfield, Dale. Quality Control, A Practical Approach, Prentice Hall, NY, NY 1979.

Brint, Steven and Karabel, Jerome. The Diverted Dream: Community Colleges and the Promise of Educational Opportunity in America, 1900-1985. Oxford University Press, NY, NY, 1989.

Cornesky, Baker, Cavanaugh. Deming: New Directions for Improving Quality, Public Acceptance and Competitive Positioning in Colleges and Universities, Eric Document Clearing House, Alexandria, VA, 1989.

Deming, Edwards W. Quality, Productivity, and Competitive Position, 1982.

Fuch, Jerome H. Administering the Quality Control Factors, Prentice Hall, NY, NY 1979.

Glasser, William. "The Quality School", Phi Delta Kappa, February, Bloomington, IN, 1990.

Hansen, Bertrand L. Quality Control and Application, Prentice Hall, NY, NY, 1987.

Heslep, Robert D. Education in Democracy: Educations Moral Role in the Democratic State, Iowa State University Press, Ames, IA, 1989.

Harris, John. Project Cooperation: Assessing Institutional Effectiveness, Quality Improvement and the Global Picture, American Association of Community and Junior Colleges, Washington, DC, 1989.

Ishikowa, Kaoru. Guide to Quality Control, Asian Productivity Organization, Los Angeles, CA, 1984.

Imai, Masaaki. Kaizen, The Key to Japan's Competitive Success. McGraw Hill, NY, NY, 1984.

Juram, J.M. Quality Planning and Analysis, McGraw Hill, NY, NY, 1970.

Lindeman, E.C. The Meaning of Adult Education, Harvest House Ltd., Boston, MA, 1961.

Moore, W.N. Guide for Reducing Quality Controls, American Society for Quality Control, Milwaukee, WI, 1977.

Nishiyama, -Kazuo. Japanese Quality Control Circles, International Communications Association, Dallas, TX, 1981.

CHAPTER SIX

SERVICE QUALITY ADVANCEMENT AT ITS BEST
Walter A. Cameron

The journey to service quality is rewarding for customers and employees of service organizations. This chapter presents examples of how service companies are improving quality and suggests a model for insuring continuous improvements.

Service quality affects all organizations since every organization has a service function. Whether an organization is large or small, attempting to compete solely on the basis of product or price is insufficient. The key is service--attention to the customer. Existing information reveals that service quality is important, whether the product is tangible or intangible (Rosander, 1989).

SERVICE QUALITY IMPERATIVES

The focus on service quality is not due just to competitive market conditions. For many organizations, it is important from the standpoint of avoiding lawsuits. For example, mass media such as newspapers, radio, and television are examining and enforcing norms of manner, responsiveness, and sensitivity. This effort is not just to create more loyalty, but to avoid lawsuits, which often begin with situations where individuals feel abused.

From newspaper and magazine accounts and through real experiences, individuals are becoming familiar with America's health care crisis. Health care costs have risen at twice the real rate of inflation. Health care technology is out of control, public confidence in the medical profession has decreased, and there have been incidents of public attacks on physicians and institutions caught in acts of incompetence (Berwick, 1989). As a result, health care organizations are beginning to focus on quality service.

Health care organizations are concentrating on customer relations in a manner similar to that used by hotels, but for a different reason: malpractice liability is the consequence of a situation where a patient or family perceives less than total care and concern.

Financial and insurance institutions focus on the rate of errors and omissions. Errors and omissions determine not just customer satisfaction but also liability insurance rates for those companies. A rise in errors and omission loses customers and increases costs.

Service organizations in the public sector are beginning to explore ways of improving service quality. The Internal Revenue Service is seeking ways to enhance its service image (Kolak, 1989). The Department of Defense is looking for ways to improve a variety of services in the military (Russell, 1990). Educational organizations are exploring methods for ensuring quality education (Cornesky and others, 1989).

There are clear and present dangers for not attending to service quality, just as there are obvious and compelling advantages for pursuing it. Service image clearly relates to profit margins and market share.

WAYS USED TO ENHANCE SERVICE QUALITY

A variety of sales and customer service organizations have training programs but few have a total quality program. At least five categories of training programs can achieve improvement in service quality. A brief introduction, outcomes, and pitfalls of each of the programs follow.

Sales. Development of sale skills appears to be the most popular technique for improving service quality. Customer-contact employees learn sales skills to increase the amount of each sale by cross-selling services. The better programs achieve increased customer satisfaction by demonstrating awareness of needs beyond the successful transaction. If the desired result of improved service quality is short-term, this kind of training is appropriate. However, it does not address satisfaction with the products and services, which may be a larger factor in long-term business.

Pitfalls in sales training programs vary. In non-sales cultures such as many banks, the basic notion of selling is sometimes difficult to get across. To many it is inconsistent with the institutional image. When employees practice the skills, the age-old issue of incentive arises. Without incentives, salaried and hourly workers may not take the initiative to cross-sell; with incentives, sales must not take precedence over other responsibilities.

Affective Skills. Motivational programs are particularly popular for non-exempt contact people. These programs usually consist of short (less than four hours) sessions. Outside consultants run the sessions in many cases. the program focuses on changing the attitudes of front-line workers. The resulting emotional boost rejuvenates employee attitudes toward their jobs, the company, and customers. The time and attention received in the session produce a short-term positive reaction regardless of the session content.

The major pitfall of a motivational program is the good feelings disappear quickly. A potential result may be more cynical employees, who perceive motivational programs as management hype. Motivational programs can have positive effects, but need to be supported by the skills to take action so that employees can see positive outcomes of enhanced motivation.

Courtesy Skills. Many companies have developed courtesy skill programs designed to enhance skills for handling telephone transactions, ranging from listening and probing to handling complaints. These *smile-and-dial* programs increase employee efficiency and present a positive image to customers.

As with motivational programs, employees may see the difference between what they are being told to do and what happens to them. Positive, courteous, and helpful employees experience a good deal of frustration when they perceive their practices and those practiced internally in their organization are different (Newcomb, 1989). Management's inattention to skills taught to front-line workers often communicates this message.

No doubt a courteous and helpful front-line employee does make for greater customer satisfaction. Taking responsibility for resolving customer complaints when the organization is not responsive results in stressful work for employees. The employee must deliver service in spite of the company. For courtesy skills to have maximum impact, employees need to experience positive behavior from others inside the organization. In other words, the internal actions must mirror the performance employees demonstrate to external customers.

Listening and Problem-handling Skills. Programs for these skills focus on handling irate customers. They consist of skill-based training for customer contact workers. Usually the emphasis is on handling problem customers rather than handling customers' problems. These training programs focus on managing personalities and identifying problems before they begin.

As with courtesy skills, problem-handling and listening skills are critical. When an external customer presents a problem, the employee may have to resolve that issue by requesting help. To do this he or she must clearly communicate the issue to others, figure out ways to prevent similar situations from occurring, and keep his or her supervisor informed. To resolve external customer problems effectively, employees need skills to handle complex internal transactions. To maximize the effectiveness of external problem-solving, the skills taught should be the same as for handling internal customer problems. In this way, external customers are no less human beings than co-workers, and internal demands no less important than internal demands.

Human Relation Skills. Global types of interpersonal skills provide the means to increase the ability of employees to deal with customers. Communication skills become a part of this program.

The pitfall of this type of program is that it usually involves the learning of generic interpersonal skills that do not relate to one's specific job. For human relation skills to have impact, employees need to see specific applications to their job, and the management team must exhibit similar behaviors.

CASE STUDIES OF SERVICE QUALITY AT ITS BEST

Exemplary case studies of total quality improvement programs have been difficult to locate. Service organizations have only begun to explore the full range of quality improvements which manufacturing firms pursue. Selections include service quality as practiced by a manufacturing firm, an insurance company, a bank, a joint venture between two telecommunication companies, and a hospital.

United Technologies Corporation - Pratt & Whitney Division. Vogel (1989) reports when Corporation Executive Officer, Robert F. Daniel took over, customers of Pratt & Whitney jet engines were defecting to arch rival General

Electric Company (GE). Profits were at a new low. Executives afraid to admit mistakes directed their employees like armies. All the way down the line, employees refused to take responsibility for errors.

The Pratt & Whitney Division was number one for so long its managers had forgotten that sales do not come automatically. An incident in 1983 made that painfully clear. The Air Force, one of the engine maker's biggest customers dissatisfied with Pratt's service for its two main fighters opened bidding on the approximate $1 billion contracts to GE.

The poor attitude toward customers was crippling the commercial engine division. Pratt had always been United Technologies Corporation's (UTC) leading money maker. UTC spent approximately $2 billion developing a new generation of jet engines. In 1986 customers expressed little interest in the engines since they could not get service for the engines they had. Spare parts arrived months late and engineering assistance from Pratt was difficult to obtain. When customers suggested minor changes in service or design, they received retorts instead of service.

Pratt, one master of the jet-engine market, saw orders drop in 1987 while General Electric's increased. The strongest message, however, came in December 1987, when customer Japan Air Lines (JAL) ordered more than $1 billion in engines from GE. The reason was lack of service from Pratt.

To deal with financial problems. Daniel auctioned off some assets and cut staff. He realized these were not the real problems. He had to rid the company of the complacency that had allowed GE to take away business from Pratt & Whitney. The management team decided to level UTC's autocratic structure and bring more of its employees into the decision-making process. The ultimate goal was to make the corporation responsive to its customers.

At Pratt & Whitney, eight levels of management became four. Decision-making moved down to the level of the factory floor. Field representatives at Pratt & Whitney now make decisions about reimbursing customers on warranty claims. Before, they would have to wait for approvals from several corporate management layers. Empowered workers make decisions to speed service, but the imperative goes even further. Pratt & Whitney lends some of its top engineers to customers. Change in the corporate culture occurs through training. In some classes, customers participate in gripe sessions and a problem-solving team gathered from many different departments must come up with solutions.

Pratt & Whitney went further with the campaign to improve service. Service staff in the field grew despite staff cuts in the rest of the company. Japanese Air Lines got a special service center near Tokyo to meet its needs. Field representatives approve warranty replacements on the spot, instead of waiting weeks for approval from headquarters.

Hartford Insurance Company. According to Redman (1990) the Hartford Insurance Company began its quest for service quality in the mid-70s based on the Crosby model of quality. Service quality achieved some successes but in 1988 efforts had tapered off. A new service quality improvement system emerged. This system has four components: process improvement, employee recognition, communications, and continuous education and training.

Hartford consists of 250 field offices and 18,000 employees (Redman, 1990). Hartford's past experience with improving quality demonstrated that implementation had been difficult. The renewed effort included pre-implementation activities., such as the following steps:

1. Gain support of all involved, especially top leadership.
2. Pick location to begin implementation (avoid extremes, best or worst).
3. Educate and train employees on improvement process.
4. Establish current status of location.
5. Determine present success level.
6. Set standards for improvement based on external and internal customer needs.
7. Define responsibilities of employees, first line managers, department heads, internal/external audits and executives.
8. Begin review, analysis, and adjust of process for improvement.
9. Write job/product specifications.
10. Establish measurements for monitoring improvements.
11. Establish a continuous program of education and training.

To implement the quality improvement system a quality management system was developed. The purpose of the quality management system is to identify the major problems to be solved. The new program is just now being implemented at selected test sites. The results in improvements so far promise a viable system.

Citizens and Southern National Bank of Atlanta, Georgia. Phillips (1989) reports that in late 1987 the Citizens and Southern National Bank decided to do something about quality service. The employee involvement process ,established in 1983, was not effective. The process was problem oriented and once a problem reached resolution, team members lost interest in finding other problems to solve. In addition, there was little owner-ship and involvement by management.

Phillips assumed the responsibility of developing a total quality improvement process to involve all employees, supervisors and managers. The first step was to gain senior management commitment. Bill Ballard, executive vice president made the commitment and spearheaded the development of a quality service corporate mission statement:

> *We will deliver timely, error-free, competitive services which meet or exceed the expectations of our customers--both internal and external. (Phillips, 1989, p. 15).*

The next step included the involvement of middle management which was the step requiring the greatest challenge. The managers identified a list of problems to address and then received orientation to the initial plan for the total quality improvement process. The process consists of three components: an employee suggestion program, interdepartmental work teams, and a recognition program. A steering council made up of cross-functional management teams manage the process. These teams identify process problems and review all suggestions submitted.

Suggestions may come from any employee or team. Suggestions may become the source for identifying projects for quality teams. These teams address process issues identified by the steering council. Managers may serve as an advisory to teams, or they may sponsor or lead teams. Selection of the members of a team relates to the nature of the problem.

A variety of ways enhances recognition of quality service by employees. Monthly meetings highlight the work of individuals and teams. Team members receive certificates and gifts for completion of a project that results in quality improvements. Individuals who submit acceptable ideas receive individual gifts. A quarterly newsletter identifies individuals and teams and their work. In addition, the winners of the annual excellence award for teams and individuals who contributed receive recognition at an annual reception.

The following accomplishments resulted from the quality service process at the bank.

1. The cost saving for 1988 was approximately $500,000.
2. By third quarter, 1988, error rates dropped below the goals set at the beginning of the year.
3. The volume of transactions increased up to 19 percent.
4. Two-thirds of the 600 ideas submitted for attention were accepted (Phillips, 1989, p. 18).

U.S. West, Incorporated and American Telephone and Telegraph, Incorporated. Two major telecommunications, U.S. West (USW) and American Telephone and Telegraph (AT&T) in 1988 initiated a quality improvement program. The major thrust of the program was to improve quality in their complex billing process (Steeples, 1989).

USW bills AT&T and other long distance carriers for access to their network and thereby to their customers. Research by USW revealed that a large percentage of the carriers expressed dissatisfaction with the billing of long distance service. Since there were no verifiable means to handle unresolved billing issues, resolving billings required continuous negotiations. This resulted in dissatisfied customers and excessive costs to USW in terms of resources consumed.

USW formed a quality council consisting of a cross-section of all work units involved in the billing issue. The key outcomes of the quality improvement selected by the quality council were:

1. Improve customer satisfaction.
2. Reduce rework.
3. Recover dollars.
4. Enhance employee work pride.
5. Support company business objectives. (Steeples, 1989, p. 6A15).

After USW had completed some of the preliminary planning several months of discussions resulted in AT&T agreeing to work on the project. After agreeing on the activities, the two companies selected employees from both companies to serve on the quality improvement project. Each company provided resources to support the effort.

The quality process steps used in the joint effort were:

1. Select improvement area.
2. Identify outputs and customers.
3. Determine customers' expectations.
4. Describe current process.
5. Focus on improvement opportunities.
6. Determine root causes.
7. Conduct trials and implement solutions.
8. Maintain the gains. (Steeples, 1989, p. 6A16).

The joint effort required considerable expertise in quality disciplines. Both companies were keenly aware of the political realities as well as the risks involved. Agreement was made that AT&T's quality training materials as well as their quality consultant would be used. Throughout the initial 9-month project meetings were scheduled at 13-week intervals.

After initial analysis and collection of data from customers, construction of work flow charts for understanding billing discrepancies began. To determine the root causes, work teams used cause and effect diagrams. Examples of the causes discovered in the four categories included:

1. Systems - No means to verify records between access and revenue.
   - Systems not compatible.
2. Methods - No agreed upon process, different analysis.
   - Procedures/tools.
3. Data - Data sources not identical/compatible.
4. People - Lack of knowledge between revenue, access, billing, and collection.

After the test of remedies, implementation began. Of the 36 existing gaps three major remedies resulted:

1. Development of a common billing process between both companies.
2. Identification of points where mechanized systems are not compatible and revision of same.

3. Initiation of a system to remedy the issue of insufficient knowledge for both access and revenue, and billings and claims.

Both companies have committed resources to solve the problems that remain. A system for verifying the situation on customer needs became operational. In addition, the quality improvement process will be replicated in USW's Central and Northwest Areas and in AT&T's Central Region.

USW and AT&T believe that initial efforts have improved customer satisfaction levels, expedited claim closures and provided improved current year earnings. Implications for quality and cost improvements for both companies are substantial. Results are enabling both companies to be more competitive.

Kosair Children's Hospital. Stansbury (1989) reports on what the Kosair Children's Hospital in Louisville, Kentucky is doing to improve quality. The total quality management strategy used at Kosair focuses on both philosophy and process.

The philosophy of total quality management is made up of six components:

1. Meeting the requirements - The first step is to establish clear requirements. Requirements are the expectations of both external customers and internal customers.

2. Error-free work - Error-free work results in an attitude and a personal performance standard. Employees must produce work that is right the first time and every time.

3. Manage by prevention - Prevention means identification of precautions to prevent the problems from happening. The problem must be eliminated and kept from happening again, never just fix the symptom.

4. Performance measures - Two kinds of quality performance exist: quality in fact - technical and professional standards and quality in perception - standards based on customers' expectations for the particular service.

5. Action for improvement - Action for improvement is a process for identifying the real causes of problems and developing solutions.

6. Ownership - Employee sense of ownership is a critical part of the quality process. Ownership means that employees feel responsible for the things that happen in an organization.

To put the philosophy of quality in action, the people at Kosair used a process consisting of the following components:

1. Mission, values, and quality policy - employees must understand the mission, values and quality policy of the hospital for quality service to happen.

2. Management commitment - Management at all levels must demonstrate the mission, values, and quality policy to all employees.

3. Organization for total quality management - The framework for managing total quality includes a policy setting and steering committee made up of top management. In addition, committees and teams of managers and other employees at all levels exist. The structure of the quality organization should allow flexibility and promote the downward movement of decision-making to employees at the lowest level.

4. Education and training - One of the major needs in implementing quality service is the training of all employees on quality practices. Training should begin first with managers and supervisors who will provide training to other employees.

5. Customers and requirements - Collect and use feedback for both internal and external customers.

6. Opportunity identification - Techniques to enable employees at all levels to identify and improve opportunities and barriers to improvements.

7. Quality improvement/quality review - A means for quality review must exist to measure, monitor, and follow up quality actions.

8. Recognition and reward - Ways of recognizing individual employees and teams exist for rewarding people for improvement efforts and for innovation in small and large successes.

9. Communications - Communication efforts require the use of traditional as well as innovative methods.

The results of the quality service process at Kosair Children's Hospital show promise. Involvement in the process has resulted in new ways of doing business and in new ways of approaching problem solving. The key results (after two years) at Kosair are:

1. All departments and medical staff sections have functioning quality improvement and quality review plans.

2. Over 5,500 ideas for quality improvement submitted by employees and more than half of these accepted for implementation.

3. The 17 quality improvement teams have made recommendations for improvements which have resulted in the following:

   a. Twenty-five percent improvement in customer satisfaction with parking.

   b. Fifteen percent improvement in customer satisfaction with emergency room service.

   c. Fifteen percent improvement in customer satisfaction with hospital billings.

   d. Reduction in number of patients leaving the emergency room without being seen from an average of 34 per month to zero.

   e. Increase in revenue of $375,000 during first year of quality program for emergency room (due to increased number of patients served).

   f. Reduced loss of revenue due to incorrect or unsubstantiated billings (savings of $750,000 first year).

   g. Increased the number of accurate dietary trays from 53 percent accurate to 92 percent accurate.

   h. Reduced the number of late dietary trays for an annual saving of $43,000 (Stanbury, 1989, pp. 8A18-8A19).

The total quality management process at NKC Hospitals is still being implemented. It is a continuous process that is never ending. Through the quality process, employee satisfaction improved while better care, provided at a lower cost to patients, resulted.

COMMON NEEDS TO BE ADDRESSED

From the analyses of service quality programs, observed or read about, there appears to be several areas of weaknesses. More significant successes could result if efforts remove these areas of weaknesses.

Management Involvement. Management behavior impacts directly on employee performance. When supervisors conduct their own affairs differently than the skills being taught to employees, the service skills lose importance. Supervisors must exhibit behaviors expected of other employees if employee behaviors are to change.

Organization-wide Application. Service quality does not happen just at the front line of an organization. Improvement in service cannot happen if the responsibility resides solely on customer-contact employees. Expecting this to happen is similar to making the materials handler responsible for the quality of products handled. When customer-oriented values exist only for front line employees, there is the risk of creating more employee frustration. If the rest of the organization does not operate with service quality in mind, then no employee will worry about service for long. In summary, service quality must exist in the organization if delivery by front line employees is to result.

Internal Customer Sensitivity. Large organizations normally do not practice total customer sensitivity. With little direct customer contact, the majority of employees lose the sense of working for the customer. Employees end up working for personal or departmental objectives that easily can conflict with organizational goals. However, some companies find that customer sensitivity defuses to all personnel if an internal customer concept is fostered. The power of this concept is that it ties everyone conceptually to the customer.

Total Quality Management. Service quality many times competes for resources with product quality, productivity, automation, sales, and other major change programs. It often ends up losing the competition. A few companies are doing something about this trend by combining all quality efforts under one system.

The outcome of product quality and service quality should be the same: satisfying customer expectations. By combining them, economies and efficiencies result. It should not matter whether a customer's satisfaction results from a product feature or a service, but that it exists.

PROPOSED MODEL FOR SERVICE QUALITY

Service quality is indicative of the nature of services desired. Customers want the following:

1. Quality service at an affordable price.
2. Minimum delay in obtaining service.
3. Service performed in a timely manner.
4. Error-free performance of services rendered.
5. Courtesy, attention, and concern.

In order for a service organization to improve service, changes must occur in the way the organization does business.

An analysis of the service organizations that have had success in implementing and maintaining a quality service program reveals components needed for a quality program. The components that must be in a total quality service organization include: (1) leadership, (2) quality management system, (3) quality process, (4) education and training, and (5) strategy for implementation.

Leadership. The impetus for quality service must come from top management if a service organization implements a quality improvement program. Deming (1982) outlines 14 points as the plan for management to exert its leadership. The essence of these points with the responsibility for each is:

Point	*Responsibility*
Constant purpose	Top management
New age	Top management
Mass inspection	Purchasing personnel
Price tag	Purchasing personnel
Finding problems	All employees
Training on the job	Training specialists, all employees
Modern methods of supervision	Training specialists, all employees
Driving out fear	All employees
Breaking down departmental barriers	All employees
Eliminating numerical goals	All employees
Eliminating numerical work standards	All employees
Removing barriers to pride in work	All employees

| Instituting a vigorous program of education and retraining | Training specialists, all employees |
| Creating management structure to push the above points | Top management |

Only top leadership can provide the approval and support needed to promote and attain quality in service across the organization. Quality service is revolutionary and implementation requires support from the top to make the necessary changes. The philosophy and the goals of the organization must reflect quality.

Top management does more than approve - they must push the quality program. They must exert constant quality leadership. They ensure that quality thinking and actions permeate every level of the organization. Without this level of commitment quality programs fail.

Quality Management System. A system which promotes a participatory management style for focusing on meeting customer expectations through continuous improvement is a must. Operation of the system is the responsibility of a quality council, which consists of top management representation and key staff members of the organization's management team. The council establishes the quality policies and provides the means for review and coordination of the quality teams. It ensures the employees are educated on quality service and arranges for time and resources necessary to do the work. It manages the selection of priority quality problems and provides for recognition and rewards.

The quality management system is the overlay management which provides for the means by which employees address Deming's 14 points. In addition, it monitors and ensures communications of quality to all work levels.

Quality Process. Although specific tools for improving quality are important, the creation of a managerial atmosphere that encourages and promotes the use of these techniques is even more crucial. An organization must train its employees not only in these skills, but also in problem-solving principles, teamwork, and group dynamics.

Successful quality improvement is fact oriented, requiring the collection, analysis, and interpretation of data. Not just any data will do, however, for numbers can obscure an issue. Three things are necessary to achieve effective problem solving: the right data, an understanding of how to apply analysis techniques, and an interpretation that takes into account the context of the service process and what exists.

Quality improvement begins with significant problems selected by the quality council. It may be best for employees to gain skills in the techniques of quality through work on improvements within their own functional area. With experience and expertise gained, employees serve on inter-departmental teams to attack bigger problems.

The process steps include the following:

1. Select improvement area.
2. Select as team members employees with proper expertise.
3. Identify outputs and customers (internal and/or external).
4. Determine customer expectations.
5. Describe current process.
6. Determine root causes using such tools as cause and effect diagrams.
7. Test solutions and implement best solutions.
8. Continue to improve.

Education and Training - Just in Time Training. A strategy for education and training is critical for a quality program. All employees need education in the broad concepts of quality and need training in the specific processes, procedures, and techniques of quality service. In addition, training provides solutions to performance related problems.

The traditional thinking of providing massive training programs for all employees on quality is costly and largely ineffective. Education and training courses planned and developed by professional training specialists are needed. Consultant trainers can be helpful for specific phases, but if training is to be effective, it must be an integral part of the organization, an on-going commitment to develop quality human resources.

Broad education on the concepts of quality is necessary for all employees, but broad-based training programs remain inefficient. The most effective training courses begin with middle management and supervisors. These individuals, with training in instructional techniques and the assistance of professional trainers, can provide quality training as needed to employees. Training will be wasteful if not delivered as needed. Training provided by individuals who know what is appropriate and who know how to instruct, coach, and evaluate ensure a basis for effectiveness.

The above training process does not negate the need for a training department; it demands it. Planning for a wide variety of relevant courses must happen. The selection and design of content must take place if effective presentation occurs. The presentation of material so that mastery occurs is a must. Monitoring of training has to be ongoing to ensure employees are learning what they need. In addition, it is necessary to monitor individuals on the job to determine if they are applying what they learned.

Thus, the training process includes determining training needs, planning courses, preparing materials, presenting timely information, and monitoring training impact. Training is a continuous process that requires updating in a timely fashion. Developments in technology, changes in customer demands, changes in the market, and changes in competition are some of the initiators that require continuous training of employees.

Strategy for Implementation. Before beginning the program to improve service it is important that pre-implementation steps be taken. An orientation program for all employees provides the start. Everyone in the organization must understand the value of service quality. They need to accept quality improvement as a continuous process.

The establishment of means for various divisions and departments to cooperate must happen before implementation. An understanding of the importance of working together to solve problems and to prevent conflicts is essential for all who provide quality service. Unless there is cooperation, understanding, and communication among all concerned, the program will not work.

An intensive analysis of all service operation needs ensures the broad-based problems emerge for study. One must know what the status is now to begin improvements. One must start with facts about the status of quality, not preconceived ideas.

Before implementation, top management must introduce the quality policies, plans, and the program's overall operation. However, top down implementation statements may leave managers, supervisors, and employees feeling indifferent or opposed to change, so top management must make extraordinary efforts to reach out to the middle and supervisory levels, for it is there that resistance to change can be most severe. As employees take increased responsibility for maintaining quality in their own roles, supervisors and middle managers may feel threatened. Upper management should reach out and demonstrate to middle managers the new methods and ways of managing that are required.

Middle managers in cooperation with supervisors have had the most success in implementation. However, they must have a leader who is knowledgeable of the quality process and who not only works well with people but is persistent.

Middle managers and supervisors, especially those who favor the use of quality control techniques and concepts can set up demonstration projects with their employees. They are in the key position to help train employees in techniques and get employees involved.

SUMMARY

Business and industrial leaders, futurists, economists, and politicians are beyond predicting the bloom of the service economy. The focus is now on the social impact and the balance of the global economy. Major concerns include how to adapt to this inevitable revolution and how to prepare to play by the new rules of the marketplace.

Service quality begins with a restless dissatisfaction with what exists. It usually starts with the leader who believes his or her organization can do better and who will provide the structure for improvement. With commitment established, the task is to design a quality system and build service quality values into every aspect of the organization.

The question is not whether any service organization can improve quality, but whether top management has the commitment. The road to quality service is long and difficult. However, trial and error methods are no longer necessary in traveling the quality route. Many service organizations have experience in improving quality service and are happy to share it.

Those organizations that move toward quality service gain customers by demonstrating service superiority and operate more cost effectively. Employee morale and demonstrated loyalty rise and employees become more productive, a factor which affects the bottom line--profits.

USES IN ADULT AND CONTINUING EDUCATION

1. Being service-oriented and customer-focused is the key to having the competitive edge.

2. Training programs that develop generic service quality skills, such as sales, motivation, and listening, are of limited value until the employees see very specific application to their jobs.

3. Adding staff in order to be more responsive to customers is worth the money.

4. Total quality improvement begins with top management's written mission statement expressing commitment to quality service.

5. All seemingly discrete parts of an organization are bound together by service to external customers and must continually manifest that bond by serving each other as internal customers.

6. Managers must lead by example.

7. Things cannot stay the same and get better. Change must occur.

8. Improvement begins with facts about service quality, not preconceived ideas.

108

REFERENCES

Bedrwick, D.M. "Applying Quality Improvement in Health Care." Proceedings of IMPRO 89, Juran Institute, Inc., Atlanta, GA, 1989, 8A1

Cornesky, R.A. and others. Deming: New Directions for Improving Quality, Public Acceptance and Competitive Positioning in Colleges and Universities. Edinboro University of Pennsylvania, January, 1989.

Deming, W.E. Quality, Productivity, and Competitive Position. Cambridge: Massachusetts Institute of Technology, Center for Advanced Engineering Study, 1982.

Desatnick, R.L. Managing to Keep the Customer. San Francisco: Jossey-Bass Inc., Publishers, 1987.

Kolak, A.H. "The Internal Revenue Service Quality Journey." Proceedings of IMPRO 89, Juran Institute, Inc., Atlanta, GA, 1989, 4A5-4A9.

Newcomb, J.E. "Management by Policy Deployment: How to Maintain Consistency Within Organizations." Quality, 1989, 28 (1) 28-30.

Phillips, C.J. "Making an Impact on Quality: Total Quality at Citizens & Southern National Bank." Quality Digest, May, 1989, 14-18.

Redman, M.T. "The Problem in is Implementation." Presentation made at the National Quality Management Conference, Chicago, IL, February 22-23, 1990.

Rosander, A.C. The Quest for Quality in Services, Milwaukee, Wisconsin: American Society for Quality Control Quality Press, 1989.

Russel, A.L. "Strategic Plan for Implementing TQM." Presentation made at the National Quality Management Conference, Chicago, IL, February 22-23, 1990.

Stansbury, J.A. "An Action Plan for Total Quality Management in a Healthcare Organization." Proceedings of IMPRO 89, Juran Institute, Inc., Atlanta, GA, 1989, 8A9-8A19.

Steeples, M. "A Service Industry Quality Breakthrough." Proceedings of IMPRO 89, Juran Institute, Inc., Atlanta, GA, 1989, 6A13-6A18.

Vogel, Todd. "Where 1990s-style Management is Already Hard at Work." Business Week, October 23, 1989, 92-93, 96, 98, 100.

CHAPTER SEVEN

DEMING WAY AT A FEDERAL GOVERNMENT
CONTRACT AGENCY
J. Michael Lewis

Service and administrative organizations require the same key element for successful implementation of quality management--strong leadership.

The principles of management outlined in Deming's 14 points apply to any type of organization. Manufacturing, service, and administrative functions differ only in the types of processes they employ, the repetition of cycles involved, and the degree to which the processes are already defined. These differences determine the extent to which statistical methods can be meaningfully applied, but they do not alter the basic requirements for managing quality. Furthermore, these differences do not change the requirements and the impact of strong leadership.

PERSPECTIVE ON SERVICE

The service sector has become a favorite target for attack in recent years. Paying customers are developing much higher expectations for services and are less likely to forgive and forget when services of poor quality and value are delivered. Customers are demanding better services and are educating themselves to become far more discriminating. They expect services to be delivered on time. They expect services to be delivered courteously and in a form that is pleasant, comfortable, pleasing, clean, healthy, safe, and even joyful. They expect the services to be thorough and complete. They expect the services to reliably do what they were intended to do, and do it right the first time. They expect the service to have true quality and value.

One indication that many of our services are not meeting these expectations is the lack of winning service organizations in the National Quality Award competition. During its first two years, 1988 through 1991, only one organization who applied in the service industry category, Federal Express, was judged by the board of examiners to be worthy of the Malcolm Baldridge National Quality Award. The lack of winners may be an indication that service organizations do not understand the criteria for a quality system as defined by the American Society for Quality Control (ASQC). If this is the case, the problem with quality in the services sector may even be greater than anticipated. If there is lack of understanding, there is lack of knowledge about the quality profession, lack of a legitimate system for managing quality, and maybe lack of quality itself. Deming would likely conclude that the problem resides with quality leadership in the service sector.

This chapter will outline a leadership strategy use by the Eastman Chemical Company (ECC) for implementing quality management principles and systems and discuss how it can be applied successfully in a service organization. However, in any type of organization, the first task of the leader is to insure that he, his staff, and his organization develop profound knowledge of the theories of total quality management and the systems for managing the quality of products and services. The ASQC embodies this country's quality experts and is a good source for help in obtaining this knowledge.

RESPONSIBILITY FOR QUALITY

Deming is a master at raising issues that cause us to contemplate and develop insight into our organizations. His favorite opener in his seminars is to merely state, "I wonder what the problems are." After allowing his audience to review the particular situations that exist in their organizations, he abruptly remarks, "It is the leader's job to know." He then puts the situations into their proper perspective to reveal that the problems are a result of poor quality. He continues to reveal that poor quality is a result of poor systems (and processes) which are a responsibility of management. Therefore, the problems are a result of poor management of the processes, and it is the leader's job to know how to get them fixed.

Deming estimates that 85 to 95 percent of all problems in an organization are managers' responsibility and can only be fixed by them. He teaches that workers are not the problem, and that applying pressure to them to get good results from poor systems only destroys their spirit: it is the leader's job to know the problems. It is the leader's job to see that they are fixed. It is the leader's job to provide systems by which the workers can produce quality products and services. The leader, therefore, is responsible for quality.

DEMING'S VIEW ON LEADERSHIP

Deming clearly communicates in his writings and seminars the importance and the intent of the leader's role. He states that a leader's job is:

1. To make work fun.
2. To provide an environment for allowing "Pride of Workmanship."
3. To foster "Intrinsic Motivation."
4. To provide help to those who need it.
5. To remove barriers in the system.
6. To provide constancy of purpose by defining direction and sticking to it with actions.
7. To know how the system is doing and how the employees are doing.
8. To provide a good process for doing work.
9. To create a critical mass to make the necessary change.
10. To train and coach and educate.
11. To predict accurately into the future and plan accordingly.
12. To make employees successful.
13. To make resources available.
14. To provide the opportunity to produce good quality that will satisfy the customers.

Although Deming is explicitly clear about what leaders should do, he leaves the determination of how to do the leading to the leaders themselves.

Within the manufacturing, service, and administrative organizations of ECC, the strategy for implementing quality management includes a very specific role for the leaders at the company and functional organization levels. The leadership role involves the following responsibilities:

1. To establish a quality policy.

2. To develop a supportive culture.
3. To implement a process for continual improvement.
4. To provide a means for employee participation.
5. To set strategic direction and select major improvement opportunities.
6. To support plans for improvement.
7. To assess progress.
8. To reinforce participation and results.

QUALITY POLICY

The leader's first role in implementing quality management in any organization is to establish and communicate a quality policy. The policy will serve as the foundation for all efforts to continually improve and will reflect the organization's strategic business intent in regard to the issue of quality. It will include a statement of goal, the general strategy for achieving the goal, and the principles which support and enable its achievement. Large manufacturing companies who have quality policies apply them to their service and administrative organizations as well as to manufacturing.

The ECC Quality Policy is strongly based in Deming's 14 points, but it also reflects philosophies on quality from other experts among the world's best. Many organizations simply adopt Deming's points as their quality policy, insisting that hybrid versions will not work. ECC senior managers and quality professionals through much study and deliberation developed a policy they believe reflects the combined best known principles from all sources including Deming. The leader's job is to commission the development of a policy that best serves his organization's needs and to establish it as a living reference for quality management implementation. The leader's job is also to know how Deming's principles are to be applied.

CULTURE

Before proceeding too much farther along with implementation, the leader should carefully assess the existing culture in the organization and decide if it is supportive of the quality policy. The culture is that set of rules, customs, perceptions, and behaviors that define the true work environment. Each organization has a culture that is peculiar and unique. The leader's job is to establish one that is best suited to applying the principles of management outlined in the Quality Policy.

The ECC Senior Management Team established a vision defining the major characteristics of a culture required to implement the ECC Quality Policy. This vision document for the ECC culture, called The Eastman Way, is being used by company leaders as a reference in their decision-making, policy setting, and improvement efforts to lead them in making changes to the existing company culture.

Many experts in managing change therefore insist that cultural improvement is a prerequisite to successful quality management implementation and that it should be done before much organizational change is attempted. An environment that welcomes change and knows how to make transitions from the old state of affairs to the new is vitally important. Trust, innovativeness, flexibility, and recognition of the need for change are as important as having the proper approach and resources to support quality improvement.

Changing the culture will create disruption and force everyone involved to reexamine their work goals, their strategies for working, and the way they organize themselves to accomplish work. This disruption will offer challenging opportunities for training and staff development. Marsick (1988, pp. 9-21) identifies some important considerations and innovative methods for helping the staff to grow and to learn in a new culture.

The training and implementation plan must be designed with careful consideration of how the existing work environment, behaviors, rules, and attitudes must be altered. If the change is too unnatural, too threatening, and too uncomfortable, and if it presents too many unaccepted conflicts with the status quo, quality management implementation will not succeed. Knowledge of these environmental characteristics and of the principles of managing change will prevent unnecessary problems. If the change is not possible with the existing culture, the culture must be changed before implementation can begin. Otherwise, resistance to the plan will create major cultural shock and will likely kill the effort.

PROCESS FOR CONTINUAL IMPROVEMENT

Implementation of the quality policy and making continual improvement will require continual change to the culture, to the work processes, and to the management systems. A leader must therefore provide a management process that will be used throughout the organization for driving continual improvement efforts. This process must accomplish the following objectives:

    (1)   Include methods consistent with the quality policy and the cultural vision

    (2)   Solicit ideas and information from the customer so that improved quality and value can be delivered back

    (3)   Select the most critical improvements to be made

    (4)   Initiate improvement projects

    (5)   Provide a problem-solving model

    (6)   Effectively allocate the limited resources of time, money and people to execute the projects

    (7)   Implement improvement ideas to processes

    (8)   Hold the gains made by process improvements

The process should be data-based: the decisions made while using it should be based on facts and data rather than on opinions and emotions. The process should also be based on the Plan-Do-Check-Act Cycle (PDCA) which Deming introduced as the Shewhart Cycle (1986, p. 88). The PDCA achieves continual improvement by running experiment after experiment to gain and apply improved process knowledge.

    The ECC Quality Management Process (QMP), developed by staff quality professionals, was provided by company leaders as a continual improvement process model along with their expectation that it be used throughout the company. But maybe even more important, they themselves were among the first to use the management process. They demonstrated their willingness to make improvements to their own jobs and to the company-wide administrative and business processes for which they serve as stewards. An ECC brochure for external customers who purchase and use end products describes the QMP as follows:

    The Quality Management Process is a managerial process to establish control and achieve continual improvement. It is the process by which we design, implement, and continually improve our management systems. The ultimate purpose is (1) to enable any organization to provide products and services that lead in quality and value as judged by the customers, and (2) to continually improve. It is based on the integration of quality principles of statistical methods, teamwork, and performance management concepts (goals, feedback, reinforcement). The Quality Management Process is divided into four major steps.

I. **Assess Organization.** This step involves taking an in-depth look at why the organizational unit exists, who it serves, what elements are critical for success, and what are appropriate measures of effectiveness. A clear understanding of the current organization and the ideal future organization is developed. Actions focus on (a) developing a mission and vision, (b) identifying the organization's key suppliers, inputs, processes, customers (internal and external), and outputs; and (c) establishing key result areas (aspects of the work which are critical for successfully meeting customer needs); and (d) defining measures of performance from the perspective of the customer. The objective is to establish a clear understanding of why the organization exists, who it serves, what value it adds, and how it functions. This exercise is particularly revealing for administrative and service functions whose direct customers are internal to the larger organization. Their services are not always perceived as delivering value to an immediate customer who should be cultivated and satisfied like external customers.

II. **Maintain Processes.** This step involves establishing and maintaining systems to meet performance levels identified by customers and to trigger needed actions. These measurements are then monitored using statistical methods. Emphasis is placed on identifying and permanently eliminating adverse causes and on providing positive reinforcement for behaviors leading to improvements.

III. **Plan Improvement.** In this step, potential problems or opportunities are selected for improvement emphasis. Opportunities for improvement come from the other steps and from customers. This block helps the organization select the right areas for improvement and the projects that will have the most impact on providing the customers with quality and value. In addition, a system to drive the improvement, including measurement, goals, improvement strategies, feedback, and reinforcement, is developed.

IV. **Do Improvement Projects.** Improvement can result from problem solving on an existing process or designing a new process. Problem solving is built on the diagnostic and remedial journeys. The diagnostic journey involves investigating and testing theories about the problem situation to determine its true cause. During the remedial journey, a suitable remedy for the problem's cause is selected and implemented. These steps will, in turn, result in an improvement which is continually monitored to maintain the improvement.

Design of new processes involves defining the purpose, design criteria, and major steps. Focusing on the right improvement projects and doing them right improves the quality and value of our products and services. This will result in improved measures and customer satisfaction. Selection criteria for projects should be established by the organization and may include cost impact, ease of execution, resource availability, group interest, probability of success, and project duration.

The QMP is used throughout ECC in production, administrative, technical, services, and managerial functions. Once processes are well defined, the methods for making continual improvement work equally well in all types of organizations. The process for continual improvement in these organizations is affected by the interdependent nature of its functions. The leader must ensure that each functional unit adopts the new philosophy and embraces the spirit of quality management. Individual units can make significant progress on their own, but they are greatly limited by the progress being made by those who support them. A critical mass of believers can often convert the unbelievers to the cause. However, until everyone is committed to and actively involved in the effort, the organization will progress at a reduced rate.

EMPLOYEE PARTICIPATION

Probably the most underutilized resource in any organization is the minds of its employees. Progressive leaders are finding new and creative ways to take better advantage of this valuable asset. The implementation strategy for improved quality must therefore include extensive education and training, increased communications, and the full participation of employees in the management process. Employees must be better developed, more effectively encouraged, and more meaningfully involved in the efforts to produce the needed changes. Leaders must develop new skills that allow employee participation and must be willing to share some of the power and control that they have so tightly held in the past.

In many companies this challenge is being addressed with employee teams. Employee teams are being allowed to identify, prioritize, and solve problems. Employee teams are being allowed to make decisions, to change policies, to implement solutions to problems, and to design new management systems. Employee teams in natural work groups are being allowed to manage their own work. Employees are being given more responsibility, more freedom, more information, and more authority. Employees are being given more opportunities to control the quality of their work, to determine the destiny of their organization, and to take pride and joy in what they do. This increased participation can only be achieved by a willful change in management style and practice by the organization's leaders.

Throughout ECC employees are participating in the quality management process on natural teams and on cross-functional teams. Natural teams consist of a supervisor and his direct reports (employees). Natural teams of first-line supervisors (shift supervisors) and their reporting process operators are working as a unit to make decisions and solve problems for their own work processes. The shift supervisors also serve on a natural team led by their area supervisor to provide information, direction, and support to the first-level natural teams. Each employee is a team member and has an equal opportunity to participate.

In addition, the natural teams are given the authority to commission temporary cross-functional teams which are assigned a special problem to solve or a specific recommendation to make. These teams are formed with employees from various organizations who have the knowledge and expertise needed to address the assigned task. They develop a recommendation, present it to the natural team for approval, and then disband. The leader's job is to nurture these teams (with coaching, patience, time, resources, and encouragement) while the teams develop and mature into productive units of the organization.

Additional keys to success are team leadership and facilitation. Supervisors who serve as team leaders will require an expanded bank of skills and knowledge in the areas of communication style, the understanding of people, group processes for problem solving and decision-making, and methods for conducting team meetings.

Some good reference sources for these skills are <u>Working Together (Productive Communication on the Job)</u> by Sherod Miller and Associates, <u>Performance Management</u> by Aubrey Daniels and Theodore Rosen, and <u>The Team Handbook</u> by Peter Scholtes and Brian Joiner.

Often organizations provide trained professionals in these areas to facilitate the team leaders until they are comfortably proficient at handling team meetings. The organizational head can provide active leadership by modeling effective team leadership for his natural team, by providing facilitators to team leaders to assist as necessary, and by serving as a coach to those team leaders who are struggling. The organization often will not take the job of quality management implementation seriously until it sees the chief executive actively leading his own team meetings on quality improvement.

The organizational head can actively lead by modeling effective team leadership skills for his/her natural team, by providing facilitators to team leaders to assist as necessary, and by serving as a coach to those team leaders who are struggling. Gagne` (1977, pp. 245-247) identifies human modeling by a respected authoritative figure as "one of the most dependable sets of events that has been found to produce changes in attitudes and behaviors." Mager (1984, pp. 69-75) agrees that "observers learn by watching and imitating others . . . (and are) more likely to imitate a model who has prestige." The organization often will not take the job of quality management implementation seriously until it sees the chief executive actively leading his/her own team meetings on quality improvement.

MAJOR IMPROVEMENT OPPORTUNITIES

In keeping with Deming's views on management (1986, p. 116), a leader's job is to know the vital few opportunities for improvement in his organization and to see that they are properly addressed. The leader must maintain contact with the customers to fully understand their needs. The leader must maintain contact with executives up the line in the organization to fully understand corporate direction and priorities. The leader must maintain contact with employees to fully understand their problems and the barriers that exist to producing good quality. The leader must understand the mission of his organization and create a vision for the future to define purpose and direction. The leader must select the themes or areas for focusing improvement efforts and organize improvement activities and resources to get the needed results. Otherwise, improvement projects may likely be misdirected and possibly even counter-productive.

The process for focusing improvement efforts at ECC is called Leadership for a Competitive Advantage and is led by the senior management team. The process for leadership includes the following steps:

1. Pinpoint Major Improvement Opportunities (MIOs) for the organization.
2. Communicate MIOs to all organization members.
3. Help teams to define their influence and to link in.
4. Commission teams to work on projects to improve influential processes.
5. Measure progress and provide feedback to all organization members.
6. Reinforce behaviors and celebrate results.

The current MIOs at ECC are Increased Sales Revenue, Decreased Cost, and Improved Customer Satisfaction. These were strategically selected by the company leaders to provide the best competitive advantage and were kept to a limited number to help create a strong focus. These themes for improvement will be kept for two to four years and then replaced as changes create new major improvement opportunities.

Extensive communications throughout the company insure that all employees know and fully understand the direction. The objective is to inform all employees what the current MIOs are, why they are important, how the company is progressing toward their improvement, how their specific team and job impact the MIOs, and what their team is doing to support the improvement effort. Administrative and service functions in ECC do extensive analyses of their outputs to identify how they influence the company MIOs. Such areas as contacts with customers, accuracy and completeness of information, timeliness and quality of indirect services, efficiency of transactions, delays and slow responses, availability of supplies, staff size, and administrative budgets ultimately have an important impact on end results.

In Japan this process is called Policy Deployment and is one of the critical leadership processes for providing world-class quality. Real continual improvement is possible only if all efforts are focused and everyone is pulling in the same direction. Only the leaders in an organization can create the planning, organization, and support to empower all employees to make improvements.

MANAGEMENT SUPPORT

Once the employees in an organization are empowered, the leadership role becomes one of management support. This role involves steering to clarify direction, delegating authority and providing approval, responding to resource needs, and coaching to sharpen skills and eliminate confusion. Sometimes support is needed to remove barriers that only the organization head has the power to do. For example, to change a policy, to reallocate resources, to remove a constraint, or to open up sacred ground.

Providing support requires a leader to stay in touch by getting frequent and meaningful feedback about what is going on throughout the organization. Formal reporting systems can provide some information that suggests a need for support. However, the method that works best for most leaders involves making frequent trips to the workplace to talk to the employees. The Japanese word for workplace is Gemba. Japanese leaders frequently ask each other, "Have you been to Gemba lately.?" Tom Peters refers to this practice as MBWA, Managing By Wandering Around. He cites the late Sam Walton, CEO of Wal-Mart, as a good example of this leadership style (1982, p. 311). Sam spent 70 percent of his time just talking to his associates (clerks, stockkeepers, cashiers, and store managers) by traveling to visit his retail and wholesale outlet stores a full 3 1/2 days per week. Some of this role is for the purpose of building employee goodwill, but it is primarily done in quality organizations to listen and to learn. Management support is simply learning what the problems and needs of the employees are and doing something about it. In Deming's terminology, it is identifying the barriers to pride of workmanship and quality and then removing those barriers.

Executives throughout ECC use several techniques to make contact with the workers and to learn what barriers to improvement stand in their way. Executive tours, visits, and goodwill audits are a few such methods. Goodwill audits involve meeting in a casual and friendly manner with employees in their work area to observe how their quality improvement effort are progressing. Attentive listening, expressing appreciation for their contributions, and identifying needs for management support are the primary objectives. Identifying problems and needs for corrective action are of minor concern.

Informal breakfast and luncheon meetings with randomly selected employees is yet another way to make contact. In addition, a "How About Some Help" form is provided in many work areas for unit teams to document barriers they face and relay them to other organizations or managers. Whatever method is used, the leader must show personal interest in quality improvement efforts, learn what the needs and barriers are, and respond to them. Without this support, employee commitment and results will fall short of expectations.

ASSESSING PROGRESS

Progress can be assessed either with internal or external resources. Internally, bottom-line performance measures and measures for MIOs can serve as indicators of progress. Baseline data is used to establish a beginning level of performance for reference. Usually key results are measured for the period just prior to the beginning of improvement efforts to set the baseline performance. In addition, a self-assessment of implementation progress on the quality policy can be performed using quality standards for the principles and methodologies that form the basis of the policy. These Have-Do Lists provide a subjective basis for assessing a team's progress in putting the ECC Quality Policy in place. They also help communicate expectations and identify areas in the management system offering the most opportunity for improved implementation.

To perform the self-asssessment, a team has to first learn the quality standards being endorsed by management. These standards communicate expectations for the management system. Using them to assess one's own team facilitates further learning and ingrains their meaning into the team members. Once understood, the standards offer a team a clear reference for guiding its implementation progress. Those aspects of quality management where actual progress has the largest discrepancy with the target become the most fertile opportunities for improvement. Actions to accomplish these improvements can then be planned and executed. This approach is repeated on a semiannual or annual basis to provide another process for continual improvement.

Some organizations obtain external services for doing these assessments. Consulting firms offer one option, and the National Quality Award (NQA) offers another. All applicants for the award are reviewed by a Board of Examiners and assessed according to their compliance with the NQA criteria and standards for world-class quality systems. Applying for the award offers a good opportunity to learn and to improve.

REINFORCEMENT

People do only that for which they receive some type of reinforcement. Daniels (1987, pp. 18-28), Gagne` (1977, pp. 245-246), and Mager (1968, pp. 46-53 & pp. 65-68) all agree that reinforcement and the "experience of success" are important aspects for the learning of attitudes. The final job of the leader is to provide the rewards necessary to encourage their employees to actively participate in the quality improvement effort. Sometimes simple recognition of an individual's or a team's contribution to organizational efforts is all that is required. The leader can do this with a pat on the back or a personalized thank you. Sometimes the act of removing barriers to pride and joy in one's work is enough. Sometimes rewarding major contributors with extra compensation or promotions is required. Sometimes disciplinary action may even be necessary for those who do not support the effort or who willfully undermine it. Change is difficult and often painful. If the proper reinforcement system is not provided by the leader, the change will be even harder to make and may never be realized.

CONCLUSION

The implementation strategy that begins, continues, and ends with strong, enlightened, active leadership will be successful. Quality management and continual improvement are processes of continual learning: learning new skills, acquiring new knowledge, learning new attitudes, and displaying new behaviors. The leader must be among the first to learn and model the attitudes and behaviors appropriate to the new philosophy. With the leader displaying a strong example of learning and application, the rest of the organization will have a clear direction to follow.

The leader must also provide sufficient resources to develop and execute an effective plan for organizational learning. Organizational excellence will only be achieved and sustained by applying the best known methods of learning for a diverse group of adults. Changing the culture and implementing a policy and process for quality management will require the extensive and enlightened education and training of everyone. Lifetime learning must become the standard for all to follow if lasting results are to be realized.

The leader must demonstrate in his/her policy setting, decision making, resource allocation, and reinforcement system a strong and constant commitment to staff education and training. The knowledge and skills of its people should be viewed as the most important asset of the organization.

Whether in a service organization, or in administration, or in production, the principles of Deming apply equally well. If an organization learns how to satisfy its customers with good quality and value, that organization will remain healthy and strong. If an organization learns how to effectively train and educate its employees, that organization will be empowered to achieve excellence. To accomplish this goal, the leader must know what the barriers are and assume the responsibility for removing them.

LESSONS FOR ADULT AND CONTINUING EDUCATION

1. Organizations' functions differ only in the types of processes used, the repetition of cycles involved, and the degrees to which the processes are defined; these differences determine the extent to which statistical methods can be meaningfully applied.

2. Potent leadership is the key to success.

3. In a competitive environment customers are more discriminating.

4. Prerequisite to the improvement of quality is that all people in the organization develop profound knowledge of the theory of quality and the systems for managing quality.

5. Problems are the result of poor management of the processes; it is the leader's job to know how to fix them.

6. Key to assessing an organization is to specify what few elements are critical to success, decide how to measure them, and implement major improvement opportunities.

7. The most under-utilized resource is the minds of the people.

8. The organization will follow a leader who is the first to set an example as a lifelong learner and behaves consistent with his/her lessons.

REFERENCES

Daniels, A.C. and Rosen, T.A., Performance Management: Improving Quality and Productivity Through Positive Reinforcement. Tucker, GA: Performance Management Publications, 1987

Brookfield, S.D., "Facilitating Adult Learning." In S.B. Merriam and P.H. Cunningham (eds.), Handbook of Adult and Continuing Education. San Francisco: Jossey-Bass, Inc., Publishers, 1989

Deming, W. E. "Methods for Management of Productivity and Quality." Conferences held in Montreal, Canada and Kingsport, TN, October 1987 and December 1988.

Deming, W. E.; Out of the Crisis. Cambridge, Mass.: MIT Center for Advanced Engineering Study, 1986.

Gagne, R.M. The Condition of Learning. New York: Holt, Rinehart and Winston, 1977

Mager, R.F. Developing Attitude Toward Learning. Belmont, Calif: David S. Lake, Publishers, 1984

Marsick, V.J. "A New Era In Staff." In V.J. Marsick (ed.), Enhancing Staff Development in Diverse Settings. New Directions for Continuing Education, No. 38. San Francisco: Jossey-Bass, In., Publishers, 1988

Peters, T. J. and Waterman, R. H., Jr. In Search of Excellence: Lessons from America's Best-Run Companies. New York: Warner Books, 1982

CHAPTER EIGHT

UPGRADING QUALITY IN A PUBLIC SCHOOL SYSTEM
Charles Tollett

Public school systems must deal proactively with the expanding perception that quality management can improve even public education.

The leading businesses and industries in the United States have adopted some form of quality management in their quest to improve their position in an increasingly competitive and global marketplace. Those who have witnessed dramatic reversals in the workplace expect no less significant results in their public schools. The complexity of social systems in place at school and the major differences between school and work have contributed to frustration; the enthusiasm to help schools apply industrial principles is alive and well in communities across America .

Management styles in business and industry come and go. School systems which try to adopt the latest practices of industries often find that they are just beginning to employ an approach which is now on the way out. This scenario results when decision makers inadequately recognize the vast differences between the two enterprises. Parents whose employers are getting great results from a change in management or operation want no less success (quality) with the schools of their community.

Sometimes "a new way of doing business" is so pervasive and significant that it can be ignored only with great peril. The move to quality management in response to Deming's work is certainly a clear example. The leadership of Kingsport (Tennessee) City Schools believes that such is the case. The decision to become active in some form of quality management was made following our analysis and evaluation of significant issues in our educational environment.

PUBLIC EDUCATION IN CRISIS

Although there is some sense of deja vu in the recent efforts to change education, no decade in the history of America has witnessed the tremendous focus on education that characterizes the 1980s. Reform rhetoric and some action dramatically changed the discourse of education. As more money and more attention are given to public education, the management and executive segments of a community and other concerned citizens deserve the assurance that the leadership of their school system understands recent management theories and practices.

Across the United States calls for reform in education led to a series of mandated "solutions" to our current crisis. The long- standing issues of equality and quality were joined with revitalized discussion of accountability. American business and industry increasingly demanded that schools "produce graduates" qualified to function in our new marketplace. High-stakes testing and wall chart comparisons naturally followed frustration with the "non-responsiveness" of public schools and the loss of U. S. dominance in the world economy.

Perhaps the most critical factor in our current crisis is related to our unwillingness or inability to alter how we see education and the world. Surely we can make the changes necessary in public education, if we just work harder and give more tests and enforce more standards on more people more often. Surely we could have used the internal combustion engine to reach the moon if we had just worked harder and improved it steadily. Kuhn (1970) explained our reluctance to accept a new paradigm in terms of our basic belief that the old system will find a way to solve its limitations. He likened a shift in paradigm to a conversion experience. Following his view of change we can realize that courage is required of practitioners who adopt a new paradigm at early stages. The decision to do so must be made on faith -- not on experience.

When we consider the twin realities that those who "run" the schools succeeded as students in them and that most people know nothing of schools operated any other way, we can understand the difficulty in making major changes in structure. When our paradigm of schools becomes "the" paradigm, paralysis is the predictable result. What a challenge it is to "persuade" those who don't believe that something can be done to step out of the way of those who are doing it!

As Kingsport City Schools' leadership team considered the national scene just described, we saw quality management as a plausible vehicle to make changes toward improved quality in a traditional system of excellence.

A QUALITY FIRST COMMUNITY

Plato noted that whatever is honored in a community will be cultivated there. The age-old question as to whether education should reflect the society it serves or seek to change it for the better is still apt. The obvious answer that it should do both suggests the balance that is necessary and desirable. Though the balance may be delicate, it is perceived as dynamic by those who would change things. In Kingsport our responsibility is to operate a school system which reflects the community values while seeking to transform our community to become an even better one. When a community embraces a commitment to Quality First, our challenge to reflect while transforming is a happy one.

Leadership From Industry. With leadership from Eastman Chemicals Division (now Eastman Chemicals Company) and Tennessee Eastman Company, the Kingsport Area Chamber of Commerce and the City of Kingsport initiated a "Quality First" program in 1985. Tri-Cities State Technical Institute (now Northeast State Technical Community College) joined the effort as a major training facility. The city and local business and industry selected teams of employees for training. The community project was underway. The goal was no less ambitious than to convince the community that quality is the first ingredient of success in public and in non-public ventures, in production and in service organizations, and in large and in small businesses.

National Center for Quality. This center, located in Kingsport, was established in 1988 to provide training in quality management and operation. The concept is comprehensive in nature and broad-based in terms of extensive involvement.

The prior experience of the greater Kingsport community with Quality Management (QM) is referenced elsewhere in this sourcebook. It is accurate to note that QM was a topic generating considerable attention in management circles in business and industry. Quality First projects are underway in both public and private sector agencies. The National Center for Quality is an emerging reality to which our community is committed.

LEARNING THE DEMING WAY

A necessary, though not sufficient, requirement for the successful adoption of any model by an organization --particularly one involving "knowledge workers" -- is a thorough study of that model. The stages and conditions of change adoption presented in the literature can be helpful. We had a lot of personalizing to do before we could intelligently face our challenge. Our initial commitment was to understand "the system," not to adopt it. This distinction was often useful as a reminder to a team member who observed that "this is not applicable to us." As we remembered that we were here to learn QM, we were able to lower the resistance and continue the project.

Back to School. Kingsport City Schools committed to the participation of our seven system administrators and one building principal to study the Deming way of quality management. The time frame for training was ten days of classes and a significant number of additional hours spent in individual and group projects over a one-year period. The training was provided through the courtesy of Tennessee Eastman and included a management team from the City of Kingsport.

Kingsport City Schools and the City of Kingsport were willing to take the medicine we were planning to market through a National Center for Quality. Identified reasons for participation were (1) commitment to lifelong learning, (2) "Quality First" as a part of the community, (3) possible value in school improvement, and (4) the willingness to model desired behavior and practices.

Managing for Excellence (ME). The specific model used in our training was adapted from Deming's work. The fourteen principles were presented by attention focused on six composite principles:

- o   Customer Satisfaction First - A school system's first objective is to satisfy customers with best value services and products through rapid response, quality, partnerships, and clearly defined needs.
- o   Respect for People - A belief in inherent worth of each person will enable (empower) each employee to contribute in a quality way characterized by lifelong learning, participation in decisions, networking, and supportive culture.
- o   Continued Improvement - A near-fanatical commitment to customer-oriented, data-based, resource-supported, systematic improvement produces increasingly favorable outcomes.

o Processes and Prevention - Quality designed into process will let prevention replace correction and promote learning versus assessing blame.

o Manage with Facts and Data - Decision-making based on facts and data will open communication channels and reward data-sharing and statistical thinking in interpretation.

o Management Leadership - Integration of management and leadership behaviors will best serve all major stakeholders and will result in constancy of purpose, vision and mission, supportive environment, appropriate balance, modeling of desired behavior, accountability, and effective focus of resources.

The ME model gives major attention to our responsibility to focus, maintain performance, and improve performance. When we focus we do the right things. When we maintain performance we do things right. We can improve performance when we do things better. The seven major tools used in the model are:

o Performance as Excellence from People through Management - Performance management is a systematic, conscious, data-based, scientific approach to improving human performance. If applied in the value context of respect for people, it can greatly improve productivity in an organization.

o QM Team Meetings - Team meetings help leader and team manage resources to achieve mission and satisfy customers. Good meetings will use QM principles (code of conduct, action plans, minutes), positive reinforcement (sincere, specific, immediate, personal), review of data, effective listening skills, and improved projects.

o Management by Walking Around - Management by walking around means spending time listening, observing, and talking with people, customers, and suppliers in their work areas.

o Statistical Thinking - Applying statistical thinking in the collection and interpretation of data can replace "gut feeling" with a more scientific method of making decisions. A process can be recognized as "out of control" before major harm is done.

o Major Improvement Opportunities - Major improvement opportunities represent projects which are deliberately selecting as the focus of resources to improve the organization. Selection of the proper project is followed by a "diagnostic journey" to identify causes beyond symptoms and a "remedial journey" to design the remedy and attain and maintain the gain.

o Measures of performance - Every organization is challenged with the issue of measuring the "right stuff." The selection of measures to be used is often a political decision.

o Measures of Performance - Every organization is challenged with the issue of measuring the "right stuff." The selection of measures to be used is often a political decision.

o Feedback - Continual and credible feedback from employees and customers is essential in an improving organization. Surveys, questionnaires, fitness for use specifications, and a variety of other feedback mechanisms will provide valuable data if properly employed.

BUSINESS OF EDUCATION

      As we evaluated the appropriateness of adapting ME to Kingsport City Schools, we had to ask and answer the questions "What is the business of education?" and "How does education differ from business?" Until these questions are faced we are not likely to answer correctly those which follow. Our experience with ME forced us to examine the similarities and the differences between education and business.

      Who Are Our Customers? Our trainers from industry quickly asserted that the customers of schools are students, but so are parents, the general public, higher education, government, and employers. Perhaps all who benefit from the service which schools provide are customers. Students are "customers" of schools as service providers and in a sense "workers" in schools as producers of knowledge work. Since students are required to attend school and most school boards establish attendance zones, do the marketplace principles of customer service apply? The concept of customer is clearly simpler in industry or in a purely service organization.

      If one accepts the ME tenet of "customer satisfaction first," one must know the meaning of "customer." As we debated the customer issue we came to recognize our students -- immature and involuntarily with us though some may be -- as one significant customer group from a larger group of customers, clients, or stakeholders to whom we must be responsive if we are to be effective. Our adult education students, with the power to vote with their feet, are customers in a marketplace context much more clearly than are our kindergarteners. Although the academic debate continues, the message of customer satisfaction first is undisputed.

The Factory Model. Though the factory model does not adequately meet the needs of American industry, some still use it for our schools. They think and speak of students as raw material, graduates as products, teachers as workers, and principals as foremen. Use of this model results in tremendously inappropriate suggestions. If our product (graduates) is to be improved, we need better raw materials (students). Parents who produce the students, however, are sending us the best they have.

If a model such as factory is necessary in today's knowledge society, we must at least shift to think of students as workers, curriculum as raw material, teachers as executives, knowledge work as product, and learning as profit. Such a shift, or a more appropriate one with a new model, would enable us to focus on outcomes versus inputs in our accountability emphasis.

The Notion of Value Added. One of the significant concepts from business currently being applied to public education is that of value added. Proposals are being enacted to reward schools and school systems for adding value. To what or to whom? An industry which does not add value to the raw material it uses is in serious trouble. Are schools to add value to our students? Or should we add employability? It's time to be cautious. Accountability models based on value added tend to compare test scores for a group of students with scores from last year to see how much value is added. Early results from this movement show heavy temptation to "teach to the test" in both acceptable and unacceptable ways. At best the test becomes the curriculum with a very narrow focus; at worst devious means could be employed to "enhance value."

Another major concern related to value added plans for funding and accountability is the increased emphasis upon competition in a society which increasingly cries out for cooperation. The mythology of improved performance through competition is seriously flawed: (1) competition increases performance only among those who believe that they have a good chance to win; (2) those who do not believe they can win will perceive competition as threatening; and (3) as the stakes of competition are increased, the tendency to "win" at all costs and by any means is encouraged. As the value of the prize is enhanced, the contest itself becomes more trivial.

If the notion of value added is to be employed, we must expand the measure to include more of the desired outcomes from a quality education.

The First Order of Business. More than two decades ago, Drucker (1969) called attention to our change in society from manual work to knowledge work. Knowledge work requires different methods of motivation, management, and measurement of productivity. To follow his lead our first order of business is to decide what business we are in. As we warmly debate our means and methods we must give more attention to the purpose of the enterprise. Consensus on means and methods is not likely in today's diverse society. Perhaps clarity would make a better goal than certainty. Strategic planning gives us a useful vehicle for focus on mission, vision, purpose, and beliefs. We gained insight into who we are and guidance for where we are going as we "hammered out" these statements.

Industrial America now realizes that education is a vital link in global competitiveness. The emphasis on the instrumental purpose -- a qualified work force -- of education is strong. The companion intrinsic purpose -- an educated citizenry -- is just as important, though not as prominently advanced. One way to enhance clarity of purpose and meaning of education -- to understand what business we are in -- is to explore some dichotomies as applied to our enterprise. As we reflect on the dichotomies of cooperation - competition, outcome - input, professionalism - prescription, effectiveness - efficiency, creating winners - sorting winners, relativism - absolutism, feminine - masculine, social - individual, and ethical -expedient,we realize that we often confuse ends and means.

Cooperation-competition analysis can show us that the international competitiveness we desire may come through cooperation in school as well as workplace. Schools may be the only places in our society where we find people working in isolation. Renewed demands for competition in school may thwart our larger goal.

The outcome-input issue is an often foggy one. If school boards and legislators would spend more effort on clear outcomes, those who work for them could deal with inputs and processes.

Although the most effective schools are those in which teachers are treated and behave as professionals, many "reforms" are prescriptive and flaunt the basic concepts of professionalism. Reformers are demanding that teachers blindly follow directives to develop creativity and independent thinking among students.

Schools have developed an entire subculture of testing, grading, and grouping for sorting winners from losers. Our new mission demands that we create winners through procedures differing from those used to sort winners and losers. There is enough room in the winner's circle for all who pursue education.

A major benefit from the evaluation of our first order of business was the improved clarity of purpose which dichotomized thinking promoted. It is now fashionable in our organization to question the probable outcome of a particular approach, to compare our walk with our talk, and to evaluate our structure against our mission. Ghandi observed that there are many ways to fail to accomplish one's mission, but the surest is to use means inconsistent with the mission.

Models and Metaphors. Models and metaphors carry the mission of an organization as they enable people to identify with a compelling vision. They also permit a comfort zone around an idea or concept that one is considering. QM downplays the importance of slogans and quotas and replaces them with "pictures" of what is important in our business -- our own version of the organizational vision. Our vision was articulated through the strategic planning process as we described our schools and system in the year 2001. We found value in deliberate attention to our culture as people share stories which identify the heroes and heroines, the preferred style of operation, and the rewarded behavior in our organization - thus experiencing and contributing to its culture.

The common wisdom that "if it ain't broke, don't fix it" is used to justify maintaining the status quo. That is acceptable in certain fixed arenas. If, however, one adopts the metaphor of gardener rather than mechanic for her work, the old adage and its wisdom are counterproductive. In the administrative and instructional components of education the ability to employ analogies, metaphors, and models to enhance perception, effect focus, and achieve purpose is receiving much attention for the potential it represents.

Public Versus Private Sector. Some clear distinctions between the processes of governance and decision-making in public school systems versus private sector agencies are present and obvious to some. In a sociological sense, business and industry tend to operate by a closed system model -- things as products, simple goals, and control of events by a person(s) in charge. Education must be viewed in terms of an open system model -- people involved in product, broad and complex goals, outcomes that are elusive and not predetermined, and no one or few clearly in charge. Some businesses and industries are opening up the system. Public education is becoming more diverse with its student customers who did not choose to be in school, broad availability of "expertise" on desired practice, heavy impact of tradition, and public tax support. The call for choice is a clear manifestation.

These and other factors suggest some adaptation of QM as it is applied in the public schools. A challenging question is raised. Is QM, with modification, the (an) appropriate management tool for improving the effectiveness of a human enterprise while promoting the proper environment for changing the behavior of people? We in Kingsport City Schools answer in the affirmative.

ADAPTING QM TO PUBLIC SCHOOL

Despite the differences noted it is apparent that public school governance can benefit from QM or from our version of ME. We chose to incorporate helpful segments of what we learned rather than to adopt the model in total. It became for us not another program but an experience and a perspective which became a part of us -- and therefore of what we do and how we do it. Specific examples of impact in this and the final section are representative but not exhaustively illustrative. We employed a strategy of commitment to understanding and practicing QM for a period of one year rather than adopting the model. This approach allowed us to avoid some tensions and fears that would otherwise be present. It required more time and energy to do our management tasks with our "new tool." The value, however, was great and we learned more than enough to justify our investment. Emerson reminded us that a mind once stretched never returns to its former condition.

Performance Management (PM). A specific adaptation of QM and some behavior-oriented psychology were adopted in some of our schools. The greatest participation and the most dramatic results were achieved at Dobyns-Bennett High School. PM is a systematic, data-based, goal-oriented, group centered approach to producing and rewarding desired behavior. Our experience is documented in <u>Performance Management</u> (1989). The systematic pursuit of excellence through team involvement was our working goal. Group goal setting, charting performance, and the use of positive reinforcement are cornerstones of the PM approach. School attendance improved by 2.27 percent to 94.49 percent during the first year of PM. Six pilot teachers -- English, mathematics, social studies, alternative school -- led efforts which resulted in better grades, higher attendance, team support, and improved self-esteem.

The DB experience with PM was widely shared within the system and beyond. More teachers within DB and system-wide have been trained in PM -- which has become a regular component of our staff development emphasis. Our model of cooperative learning also includes some of the applications featured in the PM program.

Using Facts and Data. One of the toughest demands faced in our QM experience was the deliberate and systematic use of facts and data to improve decision-making. It was surprising to recognize the small number of decisions based upon analysis of adequate facts and data. For example, we were making staffing decisions based on presented needs without sufficient information about the use of existing staff in school settings. The complex nature of education, the multiple theories in use, and the varied perspectives of team members mean that less often than our business counterparts we can conclude that the data indicate a particular action. We need better information about performance in school to properly manage the enterprise. Our system is not alone in this dilemma as we hear requests to pour more resources into programs and approaches which have no demonstrable record of performance. This must change with new demands for accountability. We must be able to demonstrate performance with data as reliable and valid as that currently available for input measures. As such information is interpreted statistically, further improvements will result, and our schools will be able to avoid the hazard of operating "out of control."

Managing by Walking Around (MBWA) has been long practiced in schools. We have upgraded our MBWA by an improved analysis of what is taking place in light of what should be taking place. We used the diagnostic journey and the remedial journey techniques on many of our problem situations to our advantage as we pursued major improvement opportunities. The flow charting of processes as part of the diagnostic journey helped our team to see beyond the obvious and to treat causes rather than symptoms. The remedial journey led us to design a remedy to address verified causes, attain the improvement, and maintain the gain. Early projects which we processed were our planning process, staff development, student attendance, and employment of staff.

More effective feedback through formal and informal surveys, questionnaires, and public forums has helped us to better understand our community. A stakeholder analysis is in the works as part of our strategic planning process.

QUALITY AS A WAY OF LIFE

Quality Defined. The very business of defining quality is a challenge to achieving it. ME defines it in terms of customer satisfaction. What satisfies many of our student customers is a day off or a chance to become disengaged from school. Robert M. Pirsig in <u>Zen and the Art of Motorcycle Maintenance</u> (1974) eloquently pursues the issue of quality. Many adolescents understand quality at their fast-food workplace, in an athletic team, or in a movie or video better than in school, social interaction, or environmental harmony. Quality seems to appear in strange places, in fleeting moments of interaction, in helping another without hope of reward, in nature, and even occasionally in school.

Quality does not have a definition that is widely accepted; it does not have a national standard. One of its pervasive characteristics is flux; it is either getting better or getting worse in every school and in every setting.Many critics say that quality cannot be measured, but it can be and it must be. We will continue our efforts to define and measure quality in terms of efficiency and excellence in meaningful experience. It is clearly more closely related to what "comes out" of schooling than to what "goes in." Aristotle warned us that quality is not an act, it is a habit.

Leadership Redefined. Most references to leadership in our society mean headship -- being in charge of something. Our leadership team has explored the challenge and has moved toward a definition like the one articulated by Robert Terry (1989), Director of the Reflective Leadership Center of the Humphrey Institute of Public Affairs -- "Leadership is the courage to bring forth and let come forth authentic action in the commons." Leadership in education must concern itself less with sifting and sorting and more with creating winners in the commons for the common good. It makes for a compelling vision. If we are to lead, we must gain the courage to overcome the fears which prevent our doing that which ought to be done.

But We're Good. The greatest difficulties faced in restructuring our schools, with the possible exception of limiting vision, will be the argument that we are already good. If our school system is excellent (and it is), and if our test scores are high, (and they are), why should we change how we do business? As we discuss this issue, the world and the demographics of our community are changing -- with increases in population occurring in groups which have traditionally not done well in school. The best school systems in America will have the greatest difficulty in recognizing the need for change. It is true in Kingsport and it may be true where you live.

Measuring the Right Stuff. As we manage with facts and data, it becomes more critical that we collect right data. As our commitment switches to creating winners rather than sifting and sorting out those who are winners, our need for data changes. We have "facts" from testing assessment and surveys that we do not need and that we need information that we do not have. We have tested our students more thoroughly than we have tested the results of the work we have been able to get them to do. School people do not have the ethical right to invade the privacy of a student to collect "information" unless we are going to use it for the benefit of the student. Present testing practice is not consistent with this statement.

If we are to help students think -- even the higher-order thinking skills (HOTS) of synthesis and evaluation -- we must accurately measure and report their and our progress. No combination of scores from present standardized achievement tests (which measure lower-order skills of recall and application) will indicate acquired HOTS. We simply must measure "the right stuff" to achieve desired results. Creativity is neither developed nor measured through routine procedures. Will it be difficult and expensive to measure the right stuff? Yes, but it will be more expensive not to do so.

Outcomes - Not Inputs. No paradigm shift in education will be as tough as the one we must make from judging education -- quality, excellence -- on the basis of inputs to evaluating on the basis of outcomes. Most major drives in education -- from buying more computers to lowering the pupil-teacher ratio -- are input oriented. Accountability and quality demand focus on outcomes.

138

Changes in the Three Rs. We are recognizing the need to change rules, roles, and relationships if we are to have the education system that we need. New alliances and partnerships must be forged. Business and industry must join hands with education. Adopt-A-School programs, though well intentioned, will not do the job. Schools are not orphans to be adopted by benevolent big brothers. They can be good partners if the partnership serves the agenda of all and the common good. Students, parents and significant others, and schools must play on the same team if we are to win the game. New patterns of decision making at the school and community level are in order. Our School Board has endorsed shared leadership and its decentralized decision-making component.

Philip Schlechty, (1989) President of the Center for Leadership in School Reform, Louisville, Kentucky, in a series of workshops in Kingsport City Schools, challenged us to review our rules, roles, and relationships. He assisted us as we evaluated our recent QM experience, our strategic planning, and our own experience in and perspective on a changing world. He challenged us to operate Kingsport schools in such a way that each student could come home each day and tell mom, dad or significant other that today he did something he couldn't do before and some big person noticed it and praised him for it. We accepted the challenge.

Mission Statement. The Strategic Planning Team and Board of Education after many hours of refining, approved the following statement of mission for our system: "The mission of the Kingsport City School System is to provide educational services to promote knowledge, attitude, skills, and habits for productive citizenship and lifelong learning." We also developed a companion vision which sees our schools and our city as learning communities dedicated to success for each learner.

LifeLong Learning. No component of Kingsport City Schools better illustrates our commitment to QM than does our Division of LifeLong Learning -- which includes our work with those younger and older than our K-12 students. An Early Childhood Learning Center (6 weeks to kindergarten), adult high school, adult basic education, Kingsport Adult Education, wellness program, and staff development make up this division. Lifelong learning reflects all seven of the ME tools and all six principles -- particularly continued improvement, management leadership, and respect for people.

Although there are only 5,600 students in K-12 programs, we have more than 10,000 adults enrolled in classes and developmental activities each year. Because we believe that every learner is a leader and every leader is a learner, staff development for all employees is planned and conducted as part of adult learning. This kind of major emphasis empowers our vision of Kingsport as a learning community.

Kingsport Paradigm for Education Progress. We have developed a paradigm to encourage our attention to the kind of leadership demanded of us in our world of change. It emphasizes the following components as desirable at every level of operation:

1. Shared Vision - mission, purpose, beliefs, climate, and culture
2. Participative Leadership - new rules, roles and relationships
3. Customer Success Orientation - creation of winners, promotion and celebration of success by students
4. Focus on Results - evaluation of performance rather than performers
5. Flexibility - time, people, space, and knowledge
6. Support System - reward for cooperation, networks, and friendship
7. Commitment to Continued Improvement and Change - beginning and ending of something major
8. Provision for Maintenance and Continuity - doing well what we have been doing.

QM has provided our system with a tremendous catalyst for responsiveness to community interest and needs in ways unforeseen at the beginning. We endorse its adaptation by other school systems where there is a serious commitment to meaning and mission. Such an approach will enable us to free schools from the hazard of being "targets of renewal" and to empower them as "centers of renewal."

ADAPTATIONS TO ADULT AND CONTINUING EDUCATION

1. While clear differences separate "businesses" and "education," they have two commonalities of paramount importance: a) the benefits of continuous improvement, and b) the vital role of people and their need to grow.
2. Adult and continuing education should both seek to reflect the society it serves and strive to change society for the better, a necessary and desirable balance.

3. Prerequisite to implementing a new system is a thorough understanding of that system by the people who will live with it.

4. The six composite principles of Deming's fourteen points are: 1) customer satisfaction first, 2) respect for people, 3) continued improvement, 4) prevention processes replace prevention, 5) manage with facts and data, and 6) integrated management and leadership.

5. Focus plus Maintain Performance equal Improve Performance: focus results in doing the right things; maintaining performance yields doing things right; and combined the harvest is improved performance.

6. Each provider of a service has customers that are both internal and external.

7. A systematic, data-based, goal-oriented, group-centered approach to producing and rewarding desired behavior is applicable to both business and education.

8. Adult and continuing educators need better data and more facts as the basis for decision-making because of the complex nature of education and the increased pressure for accountability.

9. Quality, regardless of its operational definition, is either getting better or getting worse.

10. Aristotle suggested that quality is not an act but a habit.

11. The guide to deciding what to measure must be that it can be used to help achieve improvement.

12. Rules, roles, and relationships are primary targets for change in order to improve the system.

13. Every learner is a leader and every leader is a learner.

REFERENCES

Drucker, Peter F. The Age of Discontinuity: Guidelines to Our Changing Society. Harper and Row, 1969.

Kuhn, Thomas S. The Structure of Scientific Revolutions. Chicago: University of Chicago Press, 1970.

Pirsig, Robert M. Zen and the Art of Motorcycle Maintenance. New York: Bantam Books, 1974.

Schlechty, Philip. "New Rules, Roles, and Relationships." Paper presented to Kingsport City Schools Pre-School Conference, Kingsport, Tennessee August 23, 1989.

Snyder, Gail. "Performance Management Goes to School." Performance Management Magazine, 1989, 7(2), 18-28.

Terry, Robert. "Leadership: From Skills to Authentic Engagement." Paper presented to the Institute for Development of Educational Activities, Claremont, California, July, 1989.

CHAPTER NINE

DEMING AND THE DEMISE OF AMERICAN INDUSTRY
John R. Dew

The means by which Deming delivers his message inhibits reception. His message is also incomplete because it does not fully consider culture.

Several problems occur when attempts are made to implement Deming's "profound knowledge" in the American workplace. The first barrier involves the manner in which Deming's thoughts are presented in his lectures and writing and the second concerns the incomplete nature of Deming's prescription for vitalization. These problems cause many managers to become frustrated with the medium of the message, resulting in a breakdown in the learning process. This breakdown is very unfortunate because Deming's ideas are of critical importance to the economic future of the nation. In order to be effectively utilized in the work place, educators must go beyond the technical training of statistical tools and involve workers in an emancipatory learning process.

THE MESSAGE
Deming has distilled his message down to what he calls his 14 points and the five deadly diseases of management. The 14 points appear throughout this publication.

The five deadly diseases of management (Deming, 1986) are:
1.   Lack of constancy of purpose.
2.   Emphasis on short-term profits.
3.   Evaluation of performance, merit-rating, or annual review.
4.   Mobility of management.
5.   Running a company on visible figures alone.

The 14 points build on and reinforce one another. In the decade since Deming truly emerged on the American scene, his message has fallen on deaf ears, so perhaps some attempt at condensing or paraphrasing his thoughts will be of use.

Basically, Deming offers three important messages to people in any country who want to successfully produce products and services. First, the managers must practice an enlightened approach of management that focuses on the long-term health of the organization and their communities. Second, the managers, scientists, engineers, and often the production workers and technicians need to understand the concept of variation and the use of statistical tools to guide decision-making. Third, Deming sends a powerful message about the need for companies and communities to invest in education.

Many people make the basic mistake of thinking about Deming's message as primarily concerning the use of statistical tools. While statistics is one of his three areas of emphasis, most of his writing and his admonishments deal with enlightened leadership.

Many elements of enlightened management are pointed out by Deming. Managers must look at the long-term health of the company for making operational decisions, not at quarterly dividends. Managers must be actively involved in listening to the problems in the workplace and must be leaders in constantly improving the system.
(Deming, 1982)

An enlightened manager will create an environment in which workers can take pride in their work and in which the spirit of the workplace is one of cooperation. Any practices that are barriers to achieving these goals should be eliminated, and Deming has identified several. The system of performance appraisals, slogans such as zero defects, arbitrary goals set by managers, 100% inspection, fear, turf interests, awarding work based on price, faith in gadgets, blaming the work force, emphasis on short-term profits, and many other specific problems must be completely overhauled.

Regarding the use of statistical tools, Deming points out numerous examples of how an understanding of variation common to a system can radically change one's perception of what is occurring in that system. Deming advocates learning to use statistical tools developed by Walter Shewhart to track the variation in processes and to make informed decisions based on whether or not systems are in statistical control (Shewhart, 1931). He provides many illustrations of how a knowledge of variation and statistical tools can enhance our understanding of manufacturing and service processes. Furthermore, Deming honors his colleagues in Japan who have made new contributions to the understanding of how statistical tools can be applied and integrated into our thinking processes.

However, Deming does not advocate some wholesale mindless crusade for teaching everyone how to use statistical tools. The process of introducing these tools should be controlled starting with the management and working its way into the organization.

With respect to the educational system, Deming has pointed out that a society cannot compete in an industrial or technical arena without a heavy investment in learning, both in a school system and in training in the workplace. Through his own experience as a professor, Deming has found that many of the problems encountered in the workplace are likewise embedded in the educational system. His recommendations for overhauling the classroom are just as earthshaking as his critique of industry. Deming refused to give his students grades and rejected any form of ranking of the participants' performance. He calls for teaching methods that encourage cooperation rather than competition.

Deming's greatest criticism has been leveled at the business schools, which have systematically ignored the principles of enlightened management and statistical thinking that he advocates. Obviously, part of the responsibility for the nation's inability to produce in a competitive manner is found in the curriculum of the business schools, and, with only a few notable exceptions, most business schools are producing future managers who will complete the destruction of their organizations.

PROBLEMS WITH THE MESSAGE

One of the difficulties in communicating these three basic themes can be found in the structure of Deming's lectures and books. It is not overly harsh to observe that Deming's lectures ramble and that his two major books are written in the same cadence and style of his lectures (Deming, 1982, 1986). Likewise, it would only be fair to note that in lectures he encourages people to ask questions but then responds to their questions in a manner that may damage their self-esteem. He does not drive out fear. Conversely, a sympathetic listener will respond that Deming has a great deal of passion regarding his topic and is frustrated that his message has been disregarded.

For those who embrace Deming's message, attending his lectures can be akin to a religious experience, so we do not mind the many twists and turns Deming offers along his pathway. Each time he says, "How could they know?" or "They were just doing their best," then the faithful in the audience seem ready to cheer. For those who seek Deming's profound knowledge, the hunt for the meaning of passages embedded in his chapters can

146

be akin to the study of Scripture. And the passion that Deming's ideas instill in some people causes observations that Deming's followers have almost achieved a cult status. However, for most people, the message needs to be restructured into a less daunting format.

THE FATE OF TAYLORISM

Another difficulty can be seen in the replay of the fate of scientific management. When Frederick Taylor, Henry Gantt, and others began to conceive and practice scientific management, they were soon joined by a band of fellow travelers who were eager to exploit the popularity of the new concepts for their own financial gain (Wren, 1979). The failure of scientific management can be attributed, at least partially, to the flood of profit-oriented people who misapplied the concepts, alienated organized labor, and discredited the principles of scientific management.

In a similar manner, the country is now experiencing a flood of experts who are attempting to exploit the new emphasis on quality through many gimmicks and "quick fixes." In this regard, Deming's warning about seeking "instant pudding" needs to be reiterated. There can be no shallow reform of management, no blanket teaching of statistical tools as a panacea, and no "half-baked" attempts to involve workers in false experiments in empowerment. What is needed is wholesale radical transformation of the entire system.

ALLEGORY FOR DEMING'S WORK

Perhaps Deming's contributions and a criticism of his work can best be presented in the form of an allegory. As a change agent, Deming is much like an agricultural extension agent.

Many years ago, this agent came to a county where the farmers had a fundamentally good understanding of how to farm. They recognized that the soil had to be conserved for the use of many generations. They already knew the concepts of rotating crops, and they knew how to work together to provide irrigation, build barns, and teach their children to work together. The farm agent introduced a new tool, such as a tractor, and the farmers mastered its use and incorporated it into their philosophy and body of knowledge. In fact, they even thought of new ways to use the tractor and new attachments for it. Within a few years, they had bountiful harvests and were the envy of the world.

One day the farmers from another county visit their successful neighbors and see the tractors, the wonderful fields, and the bountiful harvests. They want this success, so they call on the farm agent to teach them. Now, the farm agent discovers that these farmers have never conserved their soil and will not rotate crops because they always want to maximize this year's harvest. They cannot see the long-term implications of their actions. Furthermore, they tear down each others' barns and teach their children to care only for themselves. In this setting, the introduction of the tractor will do little good. When the farmers get a tractor, they still have not improved because their soil has eroded. So the farm agent tells the farmers that they must first learn how to farm, learn how to use tractors, and create an educational system to support these new ideas, but the farmers are unable to change.

LIMITS OF DEMING'S WORK

Deming has been wonderfully open regarding his role in assisting Japan in their economic rebound. He states that the Japanese would have made all of these strides on their own, but he was able to nudge them along. These people understood how to manage for the long-run, how to conserve their human resources, and how to educate their youth. In introducing statistical tools, Deming provided the Japanese with a great tool that they were able to use effectively because they already knew how to manage.

In America, the managers do not know how to manage for the long-run, and have never truly valued human resources. In addition, we Americans do not effectively educate our youth to work in a cooperative manner. Introducing statistical tools will do little good in light of the fundamental problem of poor management. Faced with the current recession, American organizations have fallen back to their old methods of betrayal, laying off people with 20 years of service in order to satisfy this quarter's balance sheet. The message is loud and clear. If you want a good manufacturing job in America, you had best find a Japanese company for which to work.

Here, then, is the **main criticism of Deming's work**. While he has done an excellent job of pointing out that the managers do not really understand how to manage, he rarely moves on to question why this is so. Why are we locked in to a focus on short-term profits, management-by-objectives, performance appraisals, and managing by the visible numbers? While Deming has been a master in helping people understand the workplace from a systems approach, he seldom applies a systems view in his writings to the problem of poor management. He has offered some insightful comments in this area in his lectures, but the strength of the observations seems to be dismissed by the participants as acrid side comments.

In the allegory of the farm agent, an effective agent of change would start asking why these farmers abuse their soil and destroy each others' barns. They do not do these things because they are stupid. One must look for the underlying beliefs and patterns in the society to begin to understand the driving forces that reinforce the destructive behavior. One must find ways to unfreeze the society and introduce new concepts.

This idea is the pathway that Deming's followers must now pursue. If we back away from this analysis, then America will surely be a service economy with no major industry in any sector by the end of this century. To attempt to follow Deming by focusing on teaching statistical tools alone will cause us to miss the opportunity to work on the leadership foundation on which the statistical methods must be built.

TWO MODELS FOR AMERICA

Models of how to structure a system presently exist that will allow managers to focus on the long-term health of their companies and to delight their customers. One model is the highly successful agricultural system in the United States. A second model is certainly the dynamic industrial system of Japan. Both share important features that are generally lacking in America, but that are emerging as shown in other chapters of this publication.

American Agriculture

First, note that American agriculture was brought to its knees by the drought and depression of the 1930s, just as Japanese industry was destroyed by World War II, and as American industry will be blighted by the end of this decade.

In the face of ruin, the American government rebuilt agriculture into a thriving enterprise based on joint collaboration of the government, private farmers, and the educational system. The government provides (1) control over some crops, (2) weather forecasts, (3) price supports, (4) quality control services, (5) monitoring of the sales and distribution system, and (6) active marketing of farm products in foreign countries, to name a few.

The educational system provides many forms of support, from sponsorship for Future Farmers of America to an extensive research effort at numerous universities across the nation. Agricultural research includes the search for new hybrids of crops and new types of products from around the world. The educational system teaches farmers up-to-date methods of crop rotation, soil conservation, irrigation, and market trends.

Much of this knowledge is fed from the universities through a government-sponsored network of county agricultural agents who distribute new information to farmers. Any illusion that farmers are independent people out on the prairie is hopelessly out of touch with the reality of the government-led farm economy of the United States.

Of course, the American farm system has also benefited from private companies that have introduced better tractors, but over-investment in technology has often been the ruin of farmers. After all, it does not do much good to be able to harvest a poor crop faster, just as Deming points out that automation often leads to the faster production of more scrap. Much of the controversial advancement and changes in the use of pesticides has again come about as the result of government-sponsored research.

Japanese Industry

Likewise, the Japanese manufacturing system has been developed through the cooperative efforts of the government, financial institutions, private companies, and the educational system. The schools emphasize cooperation, loyalty, the mastery of scientific and technical skills, and a work ethic. The government encourages cooperation among companies, thus leading to standardization of methods and interchangeability of parts; these steps lead to an enhanced competitive position in world markets. The government and the companies have created a system to reward long-term planning and actions that are for the greatest benefit of the nation.

American companies cry "foul" because the Japanese encourage cooperation among companies in a manner we consider to be unfair. The problem is not in the Japanese methods but in American perceptions about the value of competition over cooperation.

DIFFERENCES BETWEEN COLLABORATION AND CENTRAL PLANNING

Neither of these models should be mistaken for the disastrous model of central planning previously proposed by the Soviets. These models fall somewhere along a continuum between central planning and a totally free (everyone for themselves) market. When the point can be located on this continuum where collaboration is maximized while maintaining input for vibrant individualism and innovation then the output of the system will apparently be maximized, and that system will dominate less productive systems. Deming himself has been referred to as a "capitalist revolutionary" who is dedicated to creating long-term profit for organizations and secure employment for workers (Dobyns, 1990).

Note the certain irony that the most unhealthy part of Japan's economy is their agricultural system, which reinforces inefficient practices for political purposes. In the same manner, the stagnant American industrial system is reinforced for the ideological purposes of a political party which exalts the mythology of a free enterprise system. Thus, the American system is destined to follow the Soviet manufacturing system (which was destroyed by the opposite political ideology of central control) into oblivion.

The European Economic Community is no doubt restructuring its manufacturing base in a manner more common with the Japanese system, emphasizing common standards. The Europeans will certainly be in a better position to follow Deming's advice than America within the next three years.

A NEW MODEL FOR AMERICA

Anyone who has been working in American industry for the last ten years can surely see the incredible rate of decay of the manufacturing system. The only parts of the system that have displayed health in the last ten years have been those that were propped up by vast expenditures in weapons programs, which have sunk the nation into debt. While it is true that selected parts of some industries have sought to implement Deming's principles, little constancy of purpose can be observed as companies continue to focus on short-term goals, lay off their loyal employees, and seek to exploit the low wage earners of Mexico.

Florida Power and Light, the only American company to win the Deming Award, has apparently backed away from the Deming path for enlightened management. General Motors canceled its Fiero line, which was supposedly being operated in accordance with Deming's principles.

Even where American companies have made improvements in their quality by partial use of Deming's ideas, the Japanese have not been asleep the last decade. They are constantly seeking to improve their processes and reduce variation in their systems, both at home and in the growing number of Japanese factories located in the United States.

The answer must be found in implementing Deming's ideas, but this implementation cannot occur without several fundamental changes in the economic system. First, the Secretary of Commerce's office must begin to play a more active role in guiding industry, just as the Secretary of Agriculture's office guides the overall agricultural program. Implementing the Malcolm Baldrige Quality Award was a tiny step forward, but at least a small step in the right direction. Unfortunately, the Baldrige Award does little to encourage companies to follow Deming's enlightened management and offers no way to bring education into the system.

Second, many laws that currently prevent cooperation among companies must be changed. Deming has pointed out many examples of statutes that make it illegal for American companies to develop standards comparable to their Japanese competitors. Antitrust laws must be revised to allow for cooperation that is not designed to fix prices or take advantage of consumers.

Third, the modest steps toward encouraging ownership of businesses by their employees must be greatly expanded to foster work environments committed to long-term employment and stability for communities. The system of professional managers sent into factories to squeeze the system in order to look good in the short term must be replaced by managers who are committed to providing vision and long-term competitive position.

The conflict-based system that has defined American labor and company relations for the last 100 years must be changed. Hopefully through employee ownership of companies, the leadership style within these companies can become one of collaboration and mutual support.

The whole educational system must be reformed to teach students the value of teamwork and cooperation. The number of days spent in class needs to be increased, possibly through the use of year-round classes. The teaching of statistics needs to be revised from emphasis on statistical tests to teaching an understanding of the concept of variation. The curriculum of the business schools needs a radical overhaul to prepare a generation of people who will lead through participative methods and understanding of the long-term needs of the workplace.

It remains only a matter of time before the Japanese and the Europeans move into the few remaining bastions of American manufacturing. Without major reform, within ten years American industry will likely not be competitive in aeronautics and astronautics. Once that occurs, America will have lost its edge in defense, so the ramifications of the failure to revamp our industrial system to support Deming's philosophy will be very profound.

CHALLENGE FOR ADULT AND CONTINUING EDUCATION

Successful teaching of Deming's principles requires an understanding of adult education and the tensions which have historically existed among advocates of vocational training.

As far back as the days of David Snedden, Charles Prosser, and John Dewey, there has been a debate regarding how education related to the work place should be conducted (Miller, 1985).

In more contemporary times, worker education has tended to divide into camps around Robert Mager (1968), who focuses on the mechanics of training from a behaviorist perspective, and those who focus on the emancipatory nature of education at work.

If we pursue Mager's focus on training techniques regarding Deming's work as educators, we will focus on the best way to develop lesson plans and examples of various control charts. There are many excellent technical manuals on teaching statistical methods, such as Besterfield (1979) and Western Electric (1956). However, in an analysis of why training for quality improvement often fails, Frank Gryna (1988) has pointed out that classes which focus on the technique of specific tools often fail. Effective classes, in Gryna's opinion, should be designed around real problems in the organization which need to be solved.

While it is important for people to learn the technical skills of plotting and interpreting control charts, this learning will best occur if the design of the curriculum is built on an understanding of emancipatory education which utilizes action research and critical thinking processes.

Eduard Lindeman (1926) proposed the concept of adult learning designed around the study of real problems and situations. The statistical thinking advocated by Deming would play a crucial role in solving situation-oriented problems. Lindeman's ideas have been enhanced by many people, and are well described today as forms of action research and participatory research (Brown and Tandon, 1983).

Many successful workshops on Deming's concepts have been taught on the basis of action research principles. Florida Power and Light designed their training around the creation of team of people who would apply their new knowledge to real situations (Sterett, 1987). Martin Marietta has provided training in statistical tools which has been designed around project teams and empowered work teams. (Dew, 1987; Mandl, 1990).

The effective design of emancipatory education for quality improvement requires the educator to draw upon examples from the students' situations, and to immediately engage the learner in relevant application of the tools (Dew, 1990).

Deming's work also relates to the movement among adult educators to create situations which engage people in critical thinking, or reflective practice. Mezirow (1990) has outlined principles of critical thinking which could strongly tie to Deming's thinking processes. To comprehend the enormity of Deming's message, people must be confronted with the need to critically reassess their underlying assumptions about what it means to be a manager, a worker, and the nature of their economic system.

Stephen Brookfield (1987) has pinpointed the crucial educational issue related to reflective practice in the work place. Reflective practice leads to new awareness and threatens the status quo in factories, farms, offices, or any other organization. When people reflect on Deming's message they can achieve a new level of awareness and begin to become obsessed with the need for change. Suddenly they are awakened to the realization that there are fewer and fewer products being made in America and that manufacturing in this nation is on the brink of extinction.

This new realization can also be illustrated in the work of Paulo Freire (1985). Freire would call this learning process "conscientization," meaning the raising of a new level of consciousness. While Freire's writing has not focused on education in industry, he has offered parallel insights related to education in impoverished agricultural countries. Freire's description of a "culture of silence" among oppressed and illiterate farmers offers a chilling echo to research in America related to the alienation of workers in American industry. As workers learn to study their system they likewise begin to change the power structure of their organization, creating the possibility of resistance from managers.

Only by utilizing the best understanding of how knowledge relates to empowerment can work place educators begin to inject Deming's radical concepts into the workplace.

CONCLUSIONS

Trying to offer criticisms of Deming's work is very difficult because he has clearly given so much. Deming has been an advocate of adult education and a practitioner of adult education through hundreds of seminars he has taught. The quality of the seminars could perhaps have been enhanced. Some people have come away disappointed by Deming's gruff demeanor on the platform, and others have not been able to accept his message because the message has not always been presented in a crisp form.

Nevertheless, the ideas presented by Deming in regard to leadership, understanding of statistical tools, and education have been landmarks for the world. Adult educators have been presented with a challenge as to how to provide emancipatory learning to workers within a context of management control, which is a problem that goes all the way back to the beginnings of adult education as a concept.

It remains to be seen how America will ultimately respond to Deming's message. However, the American-owned manufacturing base will likely have to collapse before we are ready to listen and rebuild the system in a manner consistent with Deming's principles.

REFERENCES

Besterfield, Dale H. Quality Control Englewood Cliffs, New Jersey: Prentice-Hall, 1979.

Brookfield Stephen Developing Critical Thinkers San Francisco: Jossey-Bass, 1987.

Brown, L. David and Tandon, Rajesh "Ideology and Political Economy In Inquiry: Action Research and Participatory Research" Journal of Applied Behavioral Science, 1983, 19, 277-294.

Deming, W. Edwards Quality, Productivity, and Competitive Position Cambridge, Massachusetts: Massachusetts Institute of Technology, 1982.

Deming, W. Edwards. Out of the Crisis, Cambridge, Massachusetts: Massachusetts Institute of Technology, 1986.

Deming, W. Edwards. Out of the Crisis, Boston: M.I.T., 1986, pp. 24-286.

Dew, John R. "Methods for Quality Improvement Training" IMPRO 1987 Conference Proceedings Wilton, Connecticut: Juran Institute, 1987.

Dew, John R. "Education for Continuous Improvement" Tapping the Network Journal Northfield, Illinois: Quality and Productivity Management Association, 1, Summer 1990, 8-11.

Dobyns, Lloyd, "Ed Deming Wants Big Changes, and He Wants Them Fast" Quality Digest 9, September 1990, 20-32.

Freire, Paulo The Politics of Education South Hadley, Massachusetts: Bergin & Garvey, 1985.

Gryna, Frank and Juran, Joseph Quality Control Handbook New York: McGraw-Hill, 1988.

Lindeman, Eduard C. The Meaning of Adult Education Norman, Oklahoma: University of Oklahoma, 1989.

Mager, Robert Developing Attitude Toward Learning Palo Alto: Fearon Publishers, 1968.

Mandl, Vladimir "Teaming Up for Performance" Quality Digest 9, September 1990, 42-53.

Mezirow, Jack Fostering Critical Reflection In Adulthood San Francisco: Jossey-Bass, 1990.

Miller, Melvin Principles and a Philosophy for Vocational Education Columbus, Ohio: National Center for Research in Vocational Education, 1985.

Shewhart, Walter A. Economic Control of Quality of Manufactured Product New York: Van Nostrand Co., 1931.

156

Sterett, W. Kent   "Quality At Florida Power and Light" Impro 1987 Conference Proceedings Wilton, Connecticut: Juran Institute, 1987.

Western Electric Statistical Quality Control Handbook Easton, Pennsylvania: Mack Printing Co., 1956.

Wren, Daniel A. The Evolution of Management Thought New York: John Wiley and Sons, 1979.

CHAPTER TEN

LEADING THE QUALITY IMPROVEMENT GESTALT
Paul F. Fendt and G. Michael Vavrek

Quality improvement programs are successful because they have a system and implement it rigorously. Leadership is the key to being passionately systematic.

Deming's pervasive concern is that management lead the comprehensive and constant improvement of the system plus the on-going development of people as individuals and teammates. His fourteen obligations of management help implement that concern. This chapter synthesizes the preceding chapters by summarizing their key ideas in light of leadership practices identified in Kouzes and Posner's The Leadership Challenge (1987): challenge the process, inspire shared vision, enable action, model the way, and encourage the heart. The result is a system for leading the quality improvement gestalt.

LEADERSHIP

A leader challenging the process expresses a pioneering spirit, as Fendt, in Chapter Two, pointed out that Deming and Knowles did when they started advocating their theories. Leaders cause change to achieve innovations. By encouraging improvement, leaders make their primary contribution of recognizing and supporting ideas that are potentially successful; this Lewis, Chapter Seven, underscores. But, while concerned with success, effective leaders realize that failure also is a good teacher. Cavaliere, Williamson, and Cameron, (Chapters Three, Five, and Six) with their emphasis on training, spotlight that leaders are learners.

Western management must accept the challenge by learning their responsibilities and taking on leadership for change; this is Deming urging the adoption of the new philosophy. The quality process can have a profound impact on the service organization as well as in American businesses. The essence of Deming's approach can benefit service organizations is no longer the issue; this point is clearly illustrated in Chapters Three through Eight.

Let us turn, then, to what is required to create a new approach in each service industry. Leadership from the top first is needed so that leadership from within can emerge. The president, the ceo, the board chair, or whoever is acknowledged as "the boss," must adopt the new philosophy. (S)he must clearly and consistently signal that the new philosophy of quality is what the organization will live by and live with. The importance of top level doctrine is emphasized by Halverson,Williamson, Lewis, and Dew in Chapters Four, Five, Seven, and Nine.

The leader must do more than send a memorandum. (S)he must personally receive enough orientation, training, and education to make the quality statements not only "believable" but also true for the organization. (S)he must go back to school as Tollett says in Chapter Eight.

The kind of leadership needed for implementation requires that we challenge the existing process, doing away with policies and practices which inhibit or obstruct the new philosophy. These changes must be handled carefully and thoughtfully with systematic input from all levels of the staff.

The leadership required will accept Deming's point to "eliminate slogans" which may have been used to encourage compliance with former management practices. Perhaps one such slogan in a public institution of higher education is: "The state requires us to have a systematic management planning process, so this is it!" Many higher education organizations still use management-by-objectives but in an artificial and mechanical process tied to the annual budgeting cycle; this procedure can inhibit growth as illustrated by Halverson, Williamson, and Dew.

Leadership comes first from the top but then from many quarters. In continuing higher education it may next come from mainly enlightened administrators and the faculty. If the higher education organization leader does not adopt the new philosophy, then the unit head may adopt it and proceed to implement quality processes.

In Chapters Six and Seven, Cameron and Lewis indicate that leadership in service organizations may require some in-depth reflection prior to adopting the new philosophy. Some leaders will be ready to do it today; others will require time. According to the philosophers' view "...quality is synonymous with innate excellence, unanalyzable properties that we learn to recognize only through many experiences. As Vavrek points out in Chapter One, "Quality is yet to receive its final definition." Leaders must arrive at definitions for themselves. The time for accomplishing this is time well invested because superficial approaches will fall short; the leader and the people being led must honestly believe in the new philosophy. This honest belief should not be too difficult, however, because Deming's quality philosophy challenges our basic sense of truth about doing a job well, about the reason for our service organization (its mission), about pride in knowing that each effort will help fulfill our mission.

The leadership models discussed in Chapters Six and Nine illustrate the power of quality thinking. Knowles has demonstrated that applying a new philosophy can revolutionize a professional field. It may not be an exaggeration to suggest that leaders of service organizations can generate a similar phenomenon by adopting the new philosophy.

ON-GOING DEVELOPMENT OF PEOPLE AS INDIVIDUALS AND TEAMMATES

Deming's emphasis on training, education, and retraining seems to blend with Kouzes and Posner's advocacy of daring to question the steady state. Management's commitment to the on-going development of people is exhibited, in part, by instituting training on the job. However, while American management increases training expenditures, improvement remains slow because the improvement of systems is still inhibited by this attitude: "Training is for others, not my people, not me. Our problems are different and require solutions now. We must rely on our experience, not new ways that take us a while to learn." These attitudes must be turned 180 degrees when on-going development of people as individuals and teammates is taken seriously. Management must invest in employees as assets, not expenses. In Cameron's words, total quality and in-time training.

Vision means an ideal and unique image of the future; a leader must inspire a shared vision as people develop. Creating a vision and causing it to be realized constitutes leadership. The mission statement is critical according to Cavaliere, Lewis, and Tollett. Whether doing one thing 1000% better or doing 1,000 things each 1% better, leaders make things improve. But improvement does not happen just because the leader envisions it; the leader must ignite employees to make the vision their own by having their interests at heart. Managers and employees must speak the same language, which in the Deming way, means statistics.

The removal of barriers to pride in achievement melds with inspiring a shared vision. In contrast to common performance appraisal systems, which he sees as the biggest inhibitor to pride, Deming says leaders must work on helping corrective actions continue. Managers must understand that variability is natural and then use all means to continually work on reducing significant variation.

Removing barriers to pride links with the Kouzes and Posner leadership practice of enabling others to act. When employees have a sense of ownership of the vision and of empowerment to make it happen, it will happen with extraordinary results focused on major opportunities as illustrated in Chapter Eight by Tollett. Fostering collaboration, strengthening individuals, and building teams are the leader's key tasks in realizing a vision that challenges the status quo for the purpose of continual improvement. Deming's deep regard for people results in his view of management's sacred responsibility to counsel and develop people. Training, education, and retraining are crucial to the on-going improvement of individuals and consequently the organization.

Does the leader practice what (s)he preaches? Does (s)he model the way? This is the simple test used by employees to appraise management and, consequently, to decide whether leadership deserves their respectful followership. To attract respect, leaders must be clear about their own values and beliefs which, in turn, are implemented to make things happen for continual improvement; this is shown by Tollett's description of community leaders being the driving force for school improvement.

Deming emphasizes removal of barriers to pride and the importance of training united with leadership practice. Does the leader stress teamwork but allow the organization to be functionally oriented, thus causing mutually exclusive sub-unit objectives with the boss as the employee's most important customer? In contrast, Deming's way advocates group objectives and group focuses on others outside one's own organizational sub-unit. Objectives must emphasize meeting customers' needs, not as an intermediate result defined by self-limiting numbers, but through synergy, resulting from a process that identifies customers' needs, determines possible sources of improvement, recognizes who can help accomplish improvement, and develops mutual objectives. As Fendt described Knowles, the learners must be involved.

A final leadership practice fuses with continual improvement through on-going development of people: encouraging the heart, in essence, recognizing individuals' contributions and celebrating their accomplishments. Challenging the process to achieve a pioneering vision, usually a long and arduous job, often renders people disenchanted, frustrated, and exhausted. People expect their leaders to help them "keep on truck'n." Simple visible signs of encouragement show people that they can win; when the leader removes barriers to pride of achievement, it encourages the employee's heart, which, in turn, helps support initiative and risk-taking which are the keys to continual improvement. In Chapter Three Cavaliere talks about changing higher education's faculty reward system. Perhaps a more initially practical vision is to improve the continuing education reward system for faculty.

COMPREHENSIVE AND CONSTANT IMPROVEMENT

Once a quality improvement program has begun, it must be supported daily by an attitude of constant improvement. Without movement in a positive direction, the organization veers from achieving the goals of quality.

If the parent organization, of which the continuing education unit is a part, does not implement a quality philosophy, then the continuing education unit must do so alone. Leadership becomes an even greater challenge to the unit head, who must truly challenge the process of the parent organization. Hopefully, once the parent organization witnesses the benefits of quality, it may be encouraged to do the same. Modeling the way takes on a new meaning as Williamson, in Chapter Five, shows.

Inspiring a shared vision requires the leader to find the ways to spell out, to reinforce, to encourage all sub-units to adopt the quality philosophy and

162

methods. Decision-making must be shared in order to accomplish Deming's points. Sub-units must each play a major role in the new quality system. The leader may not make all the major decisions; rather those decisions must be shared, providing the necessary empowerment to each sub-unit as Halverson, Chapter Four, Tollett, Chapter Eight, and Dew, Chapter Nine, portray. Power within the organization must be comprehensively shared in order for true progress toward the quality philosophy to succeed.

The next part, constant improvement, may very well be an art. Constant improvement is an attitude put into place by the leader. Employees must catch the spirit, develop the improvement attitude, and be rewarded for doing so. The rewards are primarily internal, not external. Although doing the job better is its own reward, the leader must try to support all sub-units and employees as well. (S)he must challenge the process, inspire the shared vision, enable people to do what they must to achieve quality, model the way, and encourage the heart. Tollett's changing the 3Rs (rules, roles, and relationships) is a useful touchstone.

Creating the constant improvement attitude requires some modeling, even some teaching and some inspiration. Greater flexibility for change may be needed; sub-units may need to reorganize. A review of the organization's mission and goals may provide an excellent starting point for everyone's adopting and implementing the new philosophy. Clearly, support must be given when the constant improvement attitude requires a policy change, a reorganization of duties, or some other major alteration.

TEAMWORK

At first glance the combination of Kouzes and Posner's leadership trait of challenging the process seems incongruous with Deming's point of driving out fear. Look again. Deming advocates that everyone work effectively for the constant improvement of quality; this requires that management be willing to learn. Learning, in turn, requires risking failure while questioning the status quo; this Halverson, in Chapter Four, confronts in his focus on classroom issues. Everyone must trust that the on-going quest for improvement is more important than failure and that learning is more important than ego satisfaction based on "playing it safe" in order to assure success. Driving out fear can encourage teamwork by making it acceptable to challenge the process in order to learn how to improve quality. In

Chapters Three, Seven, and Nine, Cavaliere, Lewis, and Dew advocate that such a view must be part of the organizational culture.

Trust, as an ingredient for building teamwork, is also underscored by Deming's obligation to stop awarding business based on price tag. Standard practice in many organizations is buying where the price is lowest. Challenging the practice by establishing a long-term relationship with a single supplier based on loyalty and trust encourages teamwork toward minimizing total cost and maximizing constant improvement. Cavaliere's and Cameron's examples illustrate the point.

A leader must inspire followers to make his/her ideal and unique image of the future their own by having their interests at heart and speaking their language. The interest of everyone must be constant improvement communicated throughout the organization. Operationally defining customers' critical characteristics forms the basis for removing barriers between departments. In Chapter Five, Williamson describes the interdependence of the community college and business to underscore teamwork. Once the customers are similarly understood by everyone, a coherent effort to improve quality is far more likely. Protecting one's turf can become less important when everybody is working toward satisfying the same client; this must be further underscored by changing the routine performance review system from individual to system evaluation. Putting everyone to work synergistically, as Halverson advocates, to make a shared vision really means that leaders focus on comprehensive and constant improvement of the system. What people do defines the system; therefore the system must be the unit of analysis.

Breaking down barriers between departments and driving out fear can also be seen as key elements to teamwork when viewed from the perspective of another leadership trait: enabling action. A key result of leadership is empowering followers to collaborate as teammates throughout the organization, according to Dew in Chapter Nine. As Deming emphasizes repeatedly, management must be willing to learn from subordinates but prerequisite is management's enabling workers to teach. The reciprocal union of managers empowering workers to focus on constantly improving the system that satisfies the clients' needs and workers teaching managers about the system is essential to fostering teamwork. Workers and managers must enable each other to act, but the manager's responsibility must make it happen by being supportive.

164

Leaders must model the way, another of Kouzes and Posner's leadership traits that bonds with the Deming way. Everyone must work to accomplish the transformation to comprehensive and constant improvement through teamwork. Until trust is organization-wide and the transformation is truly achieved, workers accustomed to the old ways of being managed are likely to keep a wary eye on their leaders. Do leaders practice what they preach? Are they clear about these new values and beliefs? Is the new philosophy being carried out? Deming outlines a three-pronged aid to modeling the teamwork way: train everyone, fix management systems, and act everywhere. Everyone in and directly related to the organization must be trained in ways which yield continual improvement as Tollett's description of "back to school" emphasizes. Management systems that inhibit steady betterment must be fixed or removed. Opportunities to improve at every level should be identified and acted upon.

By modeling the way, leaders drive out fear of the new way and consequently encourage the hearts of their followers. While comprehensive and constant improvement of the system is the focal point, on-going development of people as individuals and teammates is co-requisite. People's contributions to helping improve the system and resulting quality need to be recognized and celebrated. Challenging the process to achieve a shared vision of accomplishing the transformation to a new way is usually an arduous job. People often become disenchanted, frustrated, and exhausted. Enabling people to become successful in a new way mandates that leaders pay attention to emotional nourishment by encouraging the hearts of their teammates.

CAVEAT EMPTOR

Chapter One contains a caution that bears repeating. Statistics is the language that managers and workers must share in order to constantly be improving the system that yields ever-increasing quality. Adult and continuing educators and other service sector leaders should have patience with Deming's hard data emphasis in their soft data world. The level of statistical sophistication needed depends on the complexity of the system and the definition of quality; this needs to be remembered along with his far more acceptable and far more prominent emphasis on the growth of people. The Deming way has limitations but adult and continuing educators should not "buy out" too quickly based on an over-reaction to his industrial background and statistical emphasis. The essence of W. Edward Deming's philosophy and methodology is in resonance with our beliefs and ways: Management's responsibility is to exercise leadership for the comprehensive and constant improvement of the system plus the ongoing development of people as individuals and teammates.

OBLIGATORY QUESTIONS

Deming's 14 obligations of top management cause us to point our fingers away from ourselves. But remember, when we point away from ourselves, three fingers turn back at us. By defining ourselves as top management of ourselves, our office, our unit, our division, etc., we change the focus and gain an additional benefit from the Deming way. We can ask ourselves:

1. Is the constancy of our purpose constantly in the front of our minds?
2. Have we accepted the existence of a new economic age that requires us to be leaders for change?
3. Do we implement quality as a formative not summative criterion?
4. Is every decision guided by its contribution to improving the system?
5. Do we enable people to take pride in their work by removing barriers that prevent it?
6. Does our openness to learning drive out fear of "bad news?"
7. does our focus on customers' critical characteristics enable the entire organization to work in unison to serve those needs?
8. Are numerical goals eliminated based on the understanding that individuals are not solely responsible for outcomes?
9. Do we believe that eliminating work standards will enable constant improvement of the system to be the focus?
10. Do we operationalize ourselves as leaders in terms of coaches and teachers?
11. Do we accept statistics as the language for quality improvement?
12. Is our commitment to training others and ourselves always a top priority?
13. Are we willing to move toward a single supplier for any one item on a long-term relationship of loyalty and trust?

166

14.   Is everyone getting involved in the transformation because of our changing the emphasis from individual performance reviews to systems evaluation and improvement?

THE CHALLENGE

The 1990s will not be easy . . . We will be expected to do more with less, yet know that we will be criticized (for) question(ing) the status quo . . . At the same time, society will place greater demands on us . . . (We) must be willing to question some current policies and procedures and consider some potentially controversial alternatives" (Kaplan, 1991, pg. 18). "We must permit and celebrate radical change in the ways we do our business if our leadership is going to be effective" (Smith, 1991, pg. 28).

REFERENCES

Demings, W. Edwards. Out of Crises. Cambridge, Massachusetts: Center for Advanced Engineering Study, 1989.

Kaplan, Sheila. "Maintaining Quality in the 1990s: How Will We Pay?" Educational Record, Spring 1991. Washington, D.C.: American Council on Education.

Kouzes, James M. and Posner, Barry Z. The Leadership Challenge. How to Get Extraordinary Things Done in Organizations. San Francisco, CA: Jossey-Bass, 1987.

Smith, Peter. "Beyond Budgets: Changing for the Better." Educational Record, Spring 1991. Washington, D.C.: American Council on Education.